THE AMERICAN CROPLAND CRISIS

THE AMERICAN CROPLAND CRISIS

Why U.S. Farmland is Being Lost and How Citizens
And Governments Are Trying to Save What is Left

W. Wendell Fletcher &
Charles E. Little

Illustrations by Laurel Vaughn

American Land Forum
Bethesda, Maryland

Copyright © 1982 by The American Land Forum, Inc.

Library of Congress Catalog Card Number: 81-86530 International Standard Book Number: ISBN 0-9607898-0-4

Book design by Harriet A. Wright.
Typeset and printing by Port City Press, Baltimore, Maryland.

The American Land Forum is a non-profit membership organization undertaking a sustained national-level program concerned with land resources policy. Its aims are to provide a national forum for the resolution of difficult issues pertaining to land conservation and use through a program of discussion, research, and publication; and, generally, to advance the cause of resource stewardship by seeking a broadly-based consensus concerning the enduring values of the American land.

American Land Forum, 5410 Grosvenor Lane, Bethesda, MD 20814

"Some day," old Jamie had said, "there will come a reckoning and the country will discover that farmers are more necessary than traveling salesmen, that no nation can exist or have any solidity which ignores the land. But it will cost the country dear. There'll be hell to pay before they find out."

Louis Bromfield
The Farm (1933)

Contents

Authors' Note

This book draws on research we have undertaken over the past six years on the cropland conversion issue—part of it at the Congressional Research Service of the Library of Congress where we both served, the rest for the American Land Forum under projects sponsored by foundations and government agencies. We should like to acknowledge not a little help along the way from Robert J. Gray, formerly Executive Director of the National Agricultural Lands Study and now of the American Farmland Trust, who has written a prologue to the book; R. Neil Sampson of the National Association of Conservation Districts, whose own new book, *Farmland or Wasteland*, promises to be the basic authority for the interlocking resource issues affecting American agriculture; and Robert E. Coughlin of the University of Pennsylvania, whose research on land protection techniques is as exhaustive as it is essential to the preservation of farmland.

Others we wish to thank are Jennie E. Gerard of the Trust for Public Land; Robert C. Einsweiler of the Humphrey Institute; Dennis A. White, a planner with Howard County, Maryland; C. David Loeks of Virginia Polytechnic Institute; Jeffrey Zinn and John Justus of the Library of Congress; and Ron Eber of Oregon's Land Conservation and Development Commission—all for help and encouragement on the project. Additionally, we are indebted to the Rockefeller Brothers Fund, the National Agricultural Lands Study and the Council on Environmental Quality for supporting much of the recent research and analysis that has provided the basis for this book.

There is but one substantive observation we would like to make in this note, and it concerns the book's title—*The American Cropland Crisis*. We are aware that many of our colleagues in the policy community have been at pains to avoid calling the loss of farms and farmlands a "crisis"—and indeed many have pointedly written that it is not a crisis, yet. If the meaning of crisis pertains to whether we are in imminent danger of running out of land, or food, we agree: there's still plenty of land, plenty of food. But in a world that depends on our cropland base, and for an economy as needful of overseas markets as ours, it is folly to be dilatory about protecting what Neil Sampson refers to as "the greatest body of farmland on the face of the earth." No, the crisis is not now one of acres or bushels. It is a crisis of *sense*, for our great body of farmland is being diminished at an increasing rate as recent research has made abundantly plain. The question is, if we don't muster the political energy to save our farmland, who do we suppose will do it for us? And, further, if we don't tend to it now, how is it to be accomplished later, after the land has already been converted? That's the crisis.

With all due respect to those who wish to avoid hyperbole, when *their* crisis comes, it may be too late for a remedy. But it is not too late yet, and that's why we have published this book, title and all.

W. Wendell Fletcher
Charles E. Little

Prologue

How An Issue was Raised

When I was asked to write a prologue for *The American Cropland Crisis*, I was delighted for a number of reasons. This book represents the most definitive work to date on the issue of farmland conversion. Moreover, it represents the culmination of an effort which began five years ago when Wendell Fletcher, Charles Little, Neil Sampson, myself and a handful of others, started the long and often frustrating process of bringing the loss of cropland into national focus. First it was by means of alerting the Congress to its implications, then through the National Agricultural Lands Study, and now through a rapidly growing number of agencies, institutions, and programs.

Now that the "cropland conversion issue" is so well known, it is hard to remember when—just a few years ago—we wondered if any of our colleagues in the Congress or the Executive Branch would take us seriously in our insistence that this issue was important, with national and international implications, and that it must be dealt with earnestly. This publication is a kind of capstone in that complex chain of events, and it seems an appropriate time to look back on them.

During the course of our efforts two important considerations emerged. First, the cropland conversion issue had to be brought forcefully to the attention of Capitol Hill and by that means to the general public. Secondly, if legislation was the route—and it was—we had to move very carefully. We clearly recognized we were dealing with a subject that was both complex in its own right and at the same time politically sensitive, since it involved the question of federal involvement in land use and all of the fears and misunderstandings those words conjure up.

The first step was simple and straightforward. Little suggested a Congressional Research Service-sponsored seminar. We would invite Congressmen and staff from key offices and utilize the occasion to bring the issue "out into the open" and at the same time offer the possibility of a legislative followup. The seminar was well attended and interest seemed to be strong.

During January, 1977 we put together the ingredients of the "Jeffords" bill. This was the most difficult hurdle since the legislation was to be a catalyst for a national focus on the issue, not just an add-on to existing legislation.

From then on the process was tortuous, and not ultimately successful. However, by itself, the Jeffords' bill was not as important as the mission it performed. It provided a focal point for sharpening national debate over the whole issue. It was within this context—by forcing discussion and debate through the legislative process— that we were able to create a vehicle to carry the story of the loss of farmland to American citizens. Despite National Farm Bureau opposition to the bill (along with the National Cattlemen's Association), on the grounds that it would involve the federal government in land use decisions, the bill finally—on July 19, 1978—was formally addressed by the full Agriculture Committee of the House of Representatives.

Although we anticipated a difficult time in gaining passage before the full committee we were not prepared for the thunder-bolt which struck without warning on the day of consideration. Then-Secretary of Agriculture, Bob Bergland, a good friend of Jeffords and personally supportive, sent the committee chairman—on the day of the hearing—a letter urging defeat of the legislation. In Bergland's words, "it would make the federal government a full partner in land use decisions at the local level," producing an unwarranted federal intrusion. Despite the fact that the legislation clearly did not do any such thing, this criticism, combined with Farm Bureau opposition, resulted in the committee killing the pilot programs called for in the bill by a cliff-hanging vote, 21 to 20. With the only thing left in the bill a provision for a study, Jeffords chose to withdraw the legislation.

Still, despite the trauma of losing a legislative battle after we had spent months and months concentrating on it, we had not in fact been defeated. This was merely a single battle in a much larger war. By focusing our efforts almost entirely on the legislation it was easy to forget about the steady and widespread interest that was building around the country. And in many cases this interest was being quietly translated into action. Several states and counties moved to develop and implement farmland protection programs. Others were beginning to experiment with new and innovative approaches. These activities did not become fully apparent until almost two years later during the course of the National Agricultural Lands Study when we conducted an inventory of all state and local farmland protection programs. What we did not realize in the summer of 1978 was that pressure was building within USDA and the administration—in substantial part because of widespread interest in preserving farmland created by our legislative activities—to initiate some action to protect farmland. Governors, state legislators, and local officials were asking "What's working in other states?"

Following an ALF "policy forum" on farmland in the fall of 1978, USDA made plans to establish a major federal study on the issue. By June of 1979 the $2.2 million National Agricultural Lands Study was launched, sponsored by 12 federal agencies. Now the study is complete. And as a consequence we can confidently expect new policies at all levels of government to be put in place to protect agricultural land.

And now, as you read this excellent book, *The American Cropland Crisis*, I am sure you will come to the same conclusion I did after reviewing it. It is not only well written and timely, it also lays out the issue in a way that is comprehensive and entirely persuasive for policy makers and citizens alike. I know that this book will serve as the standard work on the cropland protection issue for years to come.

Robert J. Gray
Executive Director
National Agricultural Lands Study

Part I

Losing the Land

The Coming Crisis and the
Current Response

1

The Cropland Squeeze

In 1973, U.S. Senator Henry M. Jackson made what he thought was a bold prediction: "Between now and the year 2000, we must build again all that we have built before. We must build as many homes, schools and hospitals in the next three decades as we built in the previous three centuries." This building of a second America, according to the best estimates at the time, would require the dedication of an additional 18 million acres to urban uses in a little less than three decades.[1] The projection was so unsettling that Jackson thought it substantiated his notion that the country would face a national land use crisis unless better ways were found to guide this growth. On this, he may well have been right, but his timing was off.

Even as he spoke, an unprecedented new wave of land development was unfolding across the country, as urban growth began to take a new and uncharted course into the countryside that continues to this day. No longer is the suburban fringe of large cities the place where almost all growth occurs—although here, too, growth remains rapid. It is occurring almost everywhere—in small towns and cities, and in areas once considered almost wholly rural by past perceptions of the term. And it is occurring in every region of the country, even in areas like the Northeast and the North Central states which are losing population to the Sunbelt.

In fact, land has been developed so rapidly that it took only six years—not three decades—for 18 million undeveloped acres to be urbanized. By 1967, only about 35 million acres of land had been devoted to urban and built up uses. A decade later, when the last inventory was made, the figure stood at 65 million acres, and growing. No one knows for sure how much land has been developed in the last five years but the figure probably approaches 10 million acres.

Put in graphic terms, if all the land that was built upon between 1967 and 1977 could be concentrated in one place, it would take an area larger than Ohio to contain it. Nearly all of this land was classified as agricultural before it was converted, and about a third of it was good land for crop production.[2]

Jackson can be forgiven for his lack of foresight, for virtually no one in the early 1970s was aware of just how quickly development would consume the land. Nor did many share Jackson's notion of impending crisis, and those who did would not have thought that the crisis, when it came, would have much to do with agriculture.

To most observers of the agricultural scene in the quarter century that followed World War II, the problem was not one of too little land for farming, but too much. Successive administrations, confronted with mountainous surpluses, were obliged to pay farmers to idle as much as 62 million acres in order to keep the glut from levelling commodity prices. The explanation: crop yields were increasing at unprecedented rates while, at the same time, world markets were weak.

Those that might have worried that someday there could be a price to pay for the farmer's inclination to subdivide would have found no agreement from the agricultural establishment. As recently as 1974, a Department of Agriculture report concluded that, while urban needs might require as much as 21 million acres between 1969 and the year 2000, "we are in no danger of running out of farmland."

In fact, the report asserted that increases in productivity would permit even less land to be used for crop production in the year 2000 than was the case in 1969, when U.S. farmers planted 333 million acres (including summer fallow) and harvested 286 million.[3]

Yet how quickly events would come to challenge that calm sense of assurance! The ink was not yet dry on USDA's 1974 report when U.S. agriculture—and its land base—began to be run at full speed, and the momentum has continued ever since. In 1972, American farmers were paid to idle more land than ever before, yet produced a bin-busting bumper crop. Just two years later, most of that idle land had been brought back into production, and surpluses had all but disappeared. U.S. farmers were struggling to expand production as quickly as they could in order to meet the demands of global market that, compared to the '60s, all but emptied U.S. granaries. "Nearly four-fifths of the total cropland available in this country is already in crops," warned R.M. Davis, then the Administrator of the Department of Agriculture's Soil Conservation Service, in 1976. "Plant that remaining 20 percent and our 'cropland' frontier is gone. An expanding U.S. population, coupled with growing demand for agricultural commodities abroad, makes our potential cropland figures seem very small indeed."

SCS had just completed a field survey (published in 1977 as the *Potential Cropland Study*)[4] which showed that the nation's cropland base was far more limited than had previously been believed. It had always been assumed that if times really got tough it would always be possible for farmers to bring acres from the cropland "reserve"—land with good potential for crop production that is used for woodland, pasture or range—into cultivation. Before SCS completed its survey, it was thought that 266 million acres was in this reserve category. What the SCS survey concluded was that less than half of this land should realistically be counted as reserve (or potential) cropland. And of this, only about 36 million acres could easily be brought into production without expensive preparations.

As if that were not enough, the survey showed that between 1967 and 1975, 24 million acres of rural land had been converted to urban and water uses. If so, rural land was being converted at a rate of three million acres per year—roughly three times the rate suggested by other Departmental statistics derived from the U.S. Census. And of this about one-third came from cropland.

A Challenge to Conventional Wisdom

Met by a reaction of frank disbelief on the part of most other agencies within USDA, the SCS findings on conversion set off an intra-Departmental statistical squabble that continues to this day. Those who have held to the more conservative figure for land conversion—the one based on U.S. Census figures—find it implausible that rural land conversion rates could triple in less than a decade. But, within USDA, another quite different application of Census figures was picking up an unprecedented new population trend that does much to explain why conversion rates have become so high.

After decades of rural exodus to the cities, rural areas as a whole are now growing. Moreover, they are not just growing but for the first time in 160 years, they are growing faster than metropolitan areas. This rural "turnaround," writes Calvin L. Beale, the USDA demographer who is widely credited with first identifying the trend, "looked so unlikely that first reports of it were greeted with some skepticism. But as the decade [proceeded], every source of formal data has confirmed the new trend, whether [population] estimates, sample surveys, or employment statistics."[5] With the preliminary results of the 1980 Census now in, confirmation is all but complete: Over the decade, non-metropolitan areas grew 15.4 per cent, while metropolitan areas grew just 9.1 percent. This, coupled with continuing growth in suburban counties, and migration of people to the South and West, almost certainly lies behind the higher rate of land conversion that is also now evident.

The SCS survey, coupled with the evidence of increased development in rural areas and rural growth, set off ripples. At a time of unprecedented change in U.S. agriculture, when farmers were suddenly plowing fencerow to fencerow, the conventional wisdom that urban pressures were of no import to farming began to be challenged as complacent, and wrong.

But long-standing "wisdom" dies hard, and it would not be until January, 1981, with the completion of the U.S. National Agricultural Lands Study (NALS), that the full implications of the SCS findings were more widely accepted. Conducted over an 18 month period, co-sponsored by USDA and the Council on Environmental Quality, and supported by 10 other federal agencies, the study is the most comprehensive assessment of the effects of agricultural land conversion ever conducted in this country.[6]

A Call for Action

What did the study find out? The NALS identified continuing non-agricultural demands for farmland as a matter for "national concern," and concluded that by the year 2000 it would be likely that *all* 413 million acres of existing cropland, along with *all* or *nearly all* of the 127 million acres of potential cropland, would need to be brought into cultivation.

With export demand growing, and uncertainty about future crop yields, "the economic and environmental costs of continued conversion of the nation's most productive agriculture into housing tracts, shopping centers, industrial sites, and reservoirs could be very high within 20 years."[7]

NALS settled to most everyone's satisfaction the statistical quarrel within USDA about how much agricultural land is converted each year by upholding the higher, three million acre SCS figure. But it also added a new wrinkle which, though less publicized, is probably a truer measure of the toll which urbanization is taking on farmland.

As the NALS study was winding its way through final reviews at USDA, it came face to face with what seemed to be a glaring inconsistency with the latest U.S. Census of Agriculture, which seemed to show that the amount of "land in farms" had actually increased by eight million acres between 1974 and 1978. "Seemed" is the important word here, for the Commerce Department (which conducts the Census) had, in the parlance of its statisticians, "underenumerated" land in farms. Two days before NALS released its report, a revised calculation came in: far from increasing, "land in farms" declined by 88 million acres between 1969 and 1978—an average annual rate of nearly 10 million acres per year.[8]

The decline in "land in farms" is not a measure of conversion *per se* for it includes land that may have been taken out of farm use for a variety of reasons, of which direct urbanization is only one. But it's likely that a substantial portion of that land is being taken out of farm use by speculators who anticipate its eventual development. Although the farm census recount came too late in the NALS study for its full implications to be assessed, the fact that urban pressures affect far more land than is actually converted is now well established.

Cautious and carefully worded, the NALS report is filled with qualifying "ifs": if exports continue to grow at projected rates, if revolutionary breakthroughs in agri-

culture do not occur, if conversion continues at present rates. But the message is unmistakable: the country will be risking a great deal if it continues to develop indiscriminately its most productive farmland, on which crops can be produced at less expense than on other land—especially since plenty of less productive land is available for development. NALS called on the federal government to make the protection of good agricultural land a national policy, and urged concerted action on the part of states and localities (buttressed with federal technical assistance and financial support) to carry out programs which would channel development to less productive land.

Although not without its critics, the NALS study has given the farmland protection issue a new visibility. Said John Block, sworn in as U.S. Secretary of Agriculture just after the report was released, "The National Agricultural Lands Study has built a strong case for establishing a national policy for protecting good agricultural land. I support such a policy. I support wrapping up the studies now and taking action."[9]

The Need for National Commitment

Block emphasized, as did NALS, that state and local government should take the lead in adopting programs to discourage development on prime agricultural lands. Coming from the highest agricultural official in an administration that is not especially pre-disposed to governmental action at any level, Block's statement is especially encouraging. But there is a danger that the momentum that has been so laboriously gained will slip.

After decades of extraordinary glut in many major crops, of rotting grain in elevators and cargo ships, of milk spilled out upon the ground, of cropland set aside and farmers paid not to farm, the message brought by NALS and others that urbanization is threatening the productive capacity of American agriculture will be difficult to translate into effective action.

Inevitably, farmland preservation raises the issue of land use control, and few governmental actions provoke as much controversy as those that involve land use regulation, directly or indirectly. There are many reasons for this, but probably the most basic concerns the effect of governmental restrictions on the potential value of land for development. Landowners seldom complain when public activities and investments (such as for highways, and public services) increase the value of their land. But when governmental restrictions would reduce the likelihood of future urban development (and the resulting potential for financial bonanza to property-owners) the clamor can be all but deafening.

Another difficulty concerns the need for widespread action. Right now, according to NALS, there are only about 110 counties and 167 municipalities across the country that are implementing farmland protection programs. That's more than most people expected, and local commitment to farmland protection is rising. But in a country that has 3,000 counties there is clearly a long way to go. Moreover, most of the existing programs catalogued by NALS are located in or near the major urban areas, or have been placed into effect at the insistence of just two states (Oregon and Wisconsin).

Most believe that the farmland protection movement will not get very far unless more state governments begin to take a far more active interest in protecting farmland. Although local governments make most decisions about land use control in this country, they do so because state governments have delegated this power to them. In the last decade, several states have assumed greater responsibility for land use controls—usually through guidelines to local government rather than direct state regulation. State action is politically difficult to achieve, but is probably essential if the country is to guide new growth away from farmland.

Moreover, states and localities could use some federal assistance. That was the notion that lay behind a bill, introduced by Republican Congressman James E. Jeffords of Vermont, shortly after the NALS was established. His bill, H.R. 2551, the Agricultural Land Protection Act, proposed three actions. First was a long-term study of the issue, building on the National Agricultural Lands Study to, in effect, institutionalize research on the topic, just as other natural resource research is institutionalized in the U.S. Department of Agriculture. Second was a financial and technical assistance program to help states and localities demonstrate and test methods of reducing conversion of farmland to non-agricultural uses. Third was a policy aimed at constraining federal programs and projects from vitiating state or local efforts to preserve farmland. (Federal and federally assisted public works projects often have been undertaken on prime agricultural land even when less productive acreage was available. The idea was to require such projects to be consistent with state or local farmland protection programs.)

The bill was a "cautious, responsible, moderate response to the problem," [10] said House Agriculture Committee Chairman Thomas Foley, a sentiment with which few disagreed.

Strongly supported by such organizations as the National Association of Counties and the National Association of Conservation Districts, the bill might well have passed, had the American Farm Bureau Federation not reneged on its support. Though the Farm Bureau had never been a strong proponent of the proposal, a last minute letter derogating the bill caused 13 co-sponsors among other potential allies to withhold approval. Also, the Carter White House's Office of Management and Budget kept the Department of Agriculture from supporting the measure, which it might well have done since the bill was an outgrowth of the Department's own research findings. And, ironically, the Administration had, six months before, moved independently of the legislation in establishing the National Agricultural

Lands Study, thus ostensibly obviating the need for legislation until the study's conclusion.

When it came up for debate, the Agricultural Land Protection Act was an easy target for its opponents. They argued that H.R. 2551 should await the conclusion of the Administration's study, that the "demonstration grants" were really the camel's nose of federal land use planning edging into the tent of rural property rights, that the $60 million price tag was too high at a time when almost any federal expenditure was too high. And the arguments carried the day.

A look at the bill itself would suggest that these assertions were largely disingenuous. The money issue, in the context of conservation projects and subsidies even then routinely approved by Congress, was strangely out-of-joint with the problem at hand. Moreover, the NALS, pre-scheduled to go out of business just a year after the bill was defeated, was not a substitute for long term research. (And, in fact, one of NALS' recommendations was to be that such a capability be developed.)

As for the camel's nose problem, the fear that the bill would lead to national land use planning clearly was unfounded. In fact, the language of the bill went to extraordinary lengths to show that such was not the intent. No community or state, under the bill, would have been forced to accept federal assistance, and whatever strings might have been attached tended to tie-up the federal government (which was to make its activities consistent with state and local farmland protection programs) rather than lower levels. Moreover, the bill explicitly stated that it was not to be interpreted as affecting property rights.

That debate is now history, but the question of

whether the country can muster the political will to protect one of the most important natural resources in the world is still unanswerable—despite all of the persuasive statistics and arguments now in hand which suggest that our agricultural land base is not endlessly resilient. There is still some time for effective action to be taken at various levels of government. The American cropland crisis does not lie in the current ability of U.S. agriculture to produce: it has never been more productive. Rather, it is a political crisis, one which keeps states and localities, and the federal government itself, from dealing with a problem that, left unchecked, will very likely be irremediable a decade or so from now.

For what is at stake is not simply the cropland acres thought to be directly developed, but the stability of an agricultural industry that is seeing nearly ten million acres of land dropped from the farm base each year. Much of rural America now resembles suburban America—in economy, in lifestyle, and in the sprawl that is now apparent almost everywhere. The experience of the suburbs has been, almost without exception, that when farming begins to lose its dominance in an area, its specialized rural economy and family-farm ownership structure begin to break down far in advance of actual development. Whether a similar kind of impermanence will be avoided in a growing rural America remains to be seen, but this is the environment in which a good portion of U.S. agriculture must now function if it is to function at all.

2

The Beginnings of Farmsaving:

Taxes, Districting and the Right to Farm

It all started in Maryland in 1956. The state's General Assembly, concerned about farmers going out of business and open space protection, decided to allow farms and open space lands to be assessed at a different rate than other property for tax purposes. It seemed like such a good idea that, since then, 47 other states have adopted their own programs to provide farmers and other farm landowners with property tax relief.

The notion behind the Maryland statute and other variants is a simple one. If farmers are to stay in business, and to keep their land in agriculture, they should not be expected to pay property taxes on the same basis as, say, the owner of a half-acre lot in a nearby subdivision. The problem is that farm real estate in areas subject to development pressures is worth far more for development than it is for agriculture. Without differential or preferential treatment for farmers, the farmland will be assessed for property tax purposes at the higher fair market value, and the pressure to sell will mount. By assessing farmland according to its value for agriculture, so the theory went, farmers would be encouraged to keep right on farming and, in the process, a good bit of open space greenery would be preserved.

Once the rage in open space protection circles, differential assessment has not lived up to early hopes that it would provide a cheaper way, in effect, to buy restrictive easements over farmland, or provide an alternative to zoning. In fact, if the experience of the last twenty-five years with the technique offers any single lesson, it is that differential assessment is not an easy way to skirt around the tough political issues involved in land use control.

No landowner is going to turn down property tax relief if there are no strings attached, but then the land will not be protected. With strings can come greater protection for the land, but then fewer landowners will participate voluntarily in a program. This damned if you do, damned if you don't problem with differential assessment has led to extreme dissatisfaction with the technique among farmland protection advocates. But only some of this is justified.[1] If used restrictively and in combination with other techniques such as zoning, differential assessment can help protect cropland from inappropriate conversion.

In its simplest form—usually called "preferential" assessment—the technique is little more than property tax relief for landowners (by no means all of them farmers). Eligibility is often indiscriminate (Indiana, for example, simply assesses *all* farmland in the state at its farm use value), and there are no penalties applied if the landowner subsequently develops the land.[2]

A somewhat more restrictive approach, now in use in 28 states, is called deferred taxation. Here, landowners must pay back some or all of the deferred tax (sometimes with interest) if they develop their land. But even with modest penalties imposed, few landowners are long deterred from developing their property if the price is right.

Still another approach, made famous by California's 1966 Williamson Act, is a restrictive agreement between the landowner and the government not to change the use of land. The agreement is enforceable for a ten year period once it is entered into, but getting to that point depends on the landowner. As a result, in California much of the farmland that is subject to urban pressures is not under agreement, while in rural areas the opposite is the case.

A New Generation of Incentives

More recently, some quite innovative new linkages are being forged between property tax relief and land use regulation. Some states, having lost tax revenues over the years, are now demanding a *quid pro quo.*

Nebraska, for example, allows deferred taxation only in areas zoned by counties for exclusive farm use—an approach that so far has not led area landowners to clamor for zoning, but might nonetheless dampen their opposition should zoning come to pass. Florida stipulates that landowners will no longer be eligible for tax benefits if they apply for (not necessarily receive) rezoning.

It is the state of Wisconsin, though, that is capitalizing most fully on the *quid pro quo* implied by tax relief. And it is doing so with a degree of success that few dreamed possible when the Wisconsin legislature first enacted the Farmland Preservation Act of 1977. In order for farmers to receive substantial tax benefits the law called on counties within the state to come up with agricultural zoning ordinances, or (alternatively) agricultural land preservation plans by October, 1982.

Although voluntary for the counties, the act provoked controversy in the beginning—so much so, in fact,

that the present governor campaigned against it and won.
Even so, "by the time he had established himself in
office," writes Robert E. Coughlin in a case study of the
program prepared for the National Agricultural Lands
Study, "participation had risen strongly and the program
obviously enjoyed wide popularity. The program had
evolved from a political cost to a political asset."[3]

There are no doubt many reasons for this evolution,
but most believe that the program's best selling point is
that it really does strike a fair bargain with the farmer.
The heart of the bargain is something called a "circuit
breaker tax credit." This is a complicated arrangement,
and is not, strictly speaking, an example of differential
assessment since farmers continue to pay property taxes
at the full assessment rate. Instead, the circuit breaker
allows eligible farmers to get a tax rebate on their state
income tax. The size of the rebate varies according to
how burdensome property taxes are in relation to house-
hold income. Those farmers with low incomes and high
property taxes receive the greatest rebate. Those with
higher incomes and/or lower property taxes receive the
least. In fact, since the program is not meant to be a
bonanza for the large landowner, no credits at all are
given to farmers with an income of $40,000 or more. Nor,
at the other end of the spectrum, are rebates available for
owners of less than 35 acres, or for those who have gross
farm profits of less than $6,000 per year. These latter
provisions tend to exclude most "farmettes" and many
speculative holdings.

The catch is, in order to be eligible for the circuit
breaker rebates after October 1982, the farmer's land
must be in a county that is following the state program.
For urban counties—those with more than 100 people
per square mile—this means adopting an agricultural
zoning ordinance. For rural counties this means adopting
either an agricultural land protection plan or an agricul-

tural zoning ordinance. (If they do both, farmers within the county qualify for even greater tax credits.)

In the meantime, before the 1982 deadline, farmers can qualify for some rebate by entering into contracts with the state that commit them not to develop the land for a specified period, and to manage their land according to an approved soil and water conservation plan. In addition to the tax rebates, the farmer is exempted from special assessments for sewers, water, lights, or non-farm drainage.

As an incentive to speed the counties along, rebates during the initial period are only half what they would be if the county has the zoning in effect. And if the county does not come into the program by the 1982 deadline, the farmers will not only lose eligibility for future tax credits but have to repay those already received. As an encouragement for rural counties to adopt zoning along with their plans, farmers in those counties will receive their full rebate only if zoning is in effect. (With the plan only they receive 70 percent of the entitlement.)

By giving the farmer a real stake in land use regulation, the Wisconsin program may have well broken new ground in the use of tax incentives. "Once the farmers began to receive their rebates," one public official said, "all debate about property rights stopped. Farmers no longer want to debate the land use implications of the bill. All they want us to do is help them fill out the income tax rebate form for them."[4]

There is, of course, the question of the cost that such a program entails. By 1980, with only about one third of the land area in the state participating in the program, it was not that great. If all potentially eligible farmers in Wisconsin were to participate, however, annual costs would be in the neighborhood of $80 to $100 million (or $7 to $10 per acre).

The costs may be high, but it would be ironic if the

Wisconsin law were to fail ultimately on the basis of cost. Many of the existing state differential assessment laws afford far less or even no protection for the land, and this, too, comes at a price. California's Williamson Act, for example, is thought to cost local government $18 to $36 million per year. True, it covers somewhat more land than would a fully enrolled Wisconsin program, but it actually covers less prime agricultural land. Moreover, owners of land subject to the greatest development pressure generally do not participate in the Williamson Act. What the Wisconsin program has done—something that does not come easily in this country—is to build support for land use regulation amongst the least likely constituency, the landowners themselves.

Such a constituency may be rare, but it is not accidental: the Wisconsin legislature gave farmers something they wanted—tax relief—but, by holding it at arms length, it applied a kind of *realpolitik* which eroded away a good part of the resistance of landowners and local governments to a purported infringement on their traditional hegemony on matters of land use. With a bit of resolve, on the part of legislators in other states, a new generation of tax incentives, judiciously applied and carefully linked to regulatory techniques, could very well help to solve some of the farmland protection problems that the first generation is partially implicated in creating.

Districting and the Right to Farm

If farmers in the past greeted the symptoms of agricultural impermanence—the first small then large urban encroachments that ultimately force out farming—with visions of retirement in Florida, they are more realistic about urbanization today. And with good reason. Unlike the '50s and '60s, when a farmer with a well positioned parcel of land on the fringe of a major city could count on early retirement by selling out to developers, the development today is a great deal more scattered and has pushed deeper into rural areas so that the urban fringe farmer could easily be passed over. Moreover, whether in rural Illinois or outside of Chicago, working farms and subdivisions do not make good neighbors.

To be sure, the new growth pattern has not yet brought farmers to the point of demanding that their own land be zoned for exclusive agricultural use. They *are* asserting—and forcefully so—that they have a right to farm even when lack of zoning turns the neighboring farm into a subdivision filled with people who are not inclined to be neighborly about the odors, noise, and chemicals that emanate from the fields next door.

Since 1979, when North Carolina led the way, 15 other states, in rapid fire succession, have adopted so called "right to farm" bills demanded by farmers.[5] Not surprisingly, the bills give farmers much, while demanding little. Most simply specify that local governments cannot just routinely pass nuisance ordinances against farm operations; some—as in the case of Tennessee— also provide limited exemptions to some state (but not, of course, federal) environmental requirements.

Even though the statutes assiduously avoid the issue of land use regulation, the right to farm movement is surely good news for advocates of farmland protection, for such laws are only a step away from more comprehensive approaches that protect the land as well as the right to farm it. One such approach is "districting."

"The reason I'm in the district is to protect my land from development. I want it to remain in agriculture and forestry. If people don't join agriculture and forest districts, our younger generation won't have anything to

farm. Also I want tax assessments based on use value."[6]
What this King William County, Virginia, farmer was
talking about is his state's recent (1977) agricultural districting law. First tried in New York in 1971, the districting concept has since spread not only to Virginia, but to
Maryland, Illinois, and Minnesota, where it is used in
the Twin Cities metropolitan area.

Agricultural districts may be formed in two ways.
The predominant method is initiated by the farmers
themselves. Upon approval by the county or state, the
district is established. In one state, New York, the state
government also is empowered to create districts of
2,000 acres or more if the farmland involved is considered unique or irreplaceable—a power the state has yet
to use. Once established, the boundaries of the district
are set for a fixed term, usually eight years, at the end of
which modifications will be considered.

Farmers within districts qualify for certain benefits.
Their land may be taxed on a differential basis; they
usually will not be subjected to special assessments
related to sewers, water, lights and non-farm drainage
except in so far as they use such services; state agencies
are encouraged to adopt policies and procedures that
will minimize the impact of their activities or positively
enhance farm operations in the district; local governments are forbidden to restrict or regulate farming practices unless public health and safety is concerned; and
state agency proposals for public works projects which
would affect the district must be carefully scrutinized.

In most states, farmers within districts are not prohibited from developing their land. However, in Maryland, farmers must agree not to develop their land for five
years; and in the Twin Cities, district land is zoned for
exclusive agricultural use. In Virginia and New York
county governments can legally block expansion of pub-

lic investments (such as for water and sewer lines) for development within districts, thus discouraging urbanization even though not prohibiting it outright.

At first glance, the districting approach may seem to be very little different than a glorified right to farm law. Both try to protect farmers from the "spillover" impacts of urbanization. Both are voluntary programs, with few penalties if participating farmers develop their land. And, in fact, many of the right to farm laws have simply lifted some provisions from New York's statute.

The difference—and it is an important one—is that districting does put certain obligations on the landowner and creates a sense of place for the land. "We can identify this as an agricultural area," says a Hanover County, Virginia farmer who is participating in the state program. "The people moving in know that agriculture is the predominant land use, so they won't complain about cow manure or about tractors being run."[7] Farmers in some districts have even formed associations to push for their interests. Says one observer of such an association in Livingston County, New York, "When something comes up that involves some kind of encroachment on an agricultural district, especially by public agencies, they get on it. They are not afraid to call their Congressman or write the Governor or whoever happens to be appropriate. And over a period of time the different state agencies have gotten to the point where they respect the group."

Relying primarily on the voluntary initiative and compliance of farmers, the districting approach only works when farmers really want it to. That, in itself, is quite an improvement over the days when farmers who really did want to keep right on farming in the same location had little choice but to sell out when development pressures mounted. But, while districting gives farmers staying power, it is not really an agricultural land preservation technique unless it is coupled with other measures like zoning.

The Twin Cities Approach

In the seven-county area around Minneapolis-St. Paul, that coupling is being made—through an innovative growth management strategy that aims not just to protect farmland and open space (although that is one of its objectives) but to direct new growth to the most appropriate areas. The process is overseen by a unique regional government called the Metropolitan Council, which was established by the Minnesota legislature in 1967. Unlike many regional agencies, the council has some real teeth: it sets policies for new growth, and through its control of water and sewer lines, and ability to review and modify some aspects of mandatory local planning, it often can make them stick. Yet, at the same time, actual land use planning and zoning still remains with the region's 200 local governments.

The heart of the Metropolitan Council's growth management strategy lies in the delineation of "urban service areas" and "rural service areas." Through its ability to control key public services and facilities, the council hopes to direct most new growth and development to the urban service areas, which include the Twin Cities and their suburbs, and a number of small towns scattered across the region. The rural service areas, intended to be kept agricultural for the most part, will receive much less intensive public funding for infrastructure. One estimate is that by confining public investments to the urban service areas, $2 billion will be saved over the next 15 years.

Even so, the urban and rural service boundaries are

not set in concrete. They can be modified within reason by localities, and local governments still retain exclusive authority to plan and regulate land uses within the region that do not pertain to public investments. Thus, low density development serviced by septic systems would be beyond the purview of the council. And this is where districting has come to the aid in furthering the council's growth management objectives.

About ten to fifteen percent of the region's agricultural land has been included in Urban Service Areas. As for the rest, the council would like to see it designated as long-term farming areas which would be protected from conversion through agricultural zoning. But the Metropolitan Council has no authority to require localities to adopt agricultural zoning, and some communities have been reluctant to impose zoning on landowners— especially where uncertainty exists about whether farming would continue to be economically viable.

Indeed, in many of the rural areas, there has been no small amount of uncertainty. Between 1970 and 1978, the central cities of Minneapolis and Saint Paul, and many of their older suburbs have actually declined in population, while the more rural counties increased in population by about one third. Besides direct impacts on farmland (16 percent of the region's farmland was either converted or idled in the decade between 1964 and 1974), a sense of impermanence on the part of farmers has been pervasive. Some now believe, however, that there has been a turnaround in expectations (from negative to positive) about the viability of farming in the region. As the Metropolitan Council and other government entities have made it clear that they really are serious about curbing urban sprawl, farmers have become more reluctant to sell their land to developers (in fact some are actually buying new land for cropping), and some are once more making long-term investments in improvements.[8]

In 1980, the Minnesota legislature passed a districting statute that may help to relieve any remaining uncertainty that the region is not just trying to save farmland as open space but also trying to keep agriculture economically viable. First proposed by the Metropolitan Council, the Agricultural Preserves Act now applies only to the Twin Cities region. The statute is similar to districting acts in other states, except that farmers can become eligible for benefits only if their land has been designated through the planning process for long-term farm use, and then only if the community has adopted agricultural zoning. It's too early to know how this integration of districting with land use control will turn out, but in a region that is as committed to making things work as is the Twin Cities, there is every reason for optimism.

Almost everywhere that it has been applied, the districting concept has had a stabilizing effect on agriculture—and that is its great strength. It will work best when it can be tied to zoning or other direct techniques for keeping the land in agricultural use. But even where that is not politically possible, the district may still have a great deal to offer, for it establishes agriculture and the land on which it takes place as an activity and area of importance, worthy of the respect of governments, neighbors, and indeed the landowners themselves.

3

Zoning for Food

Zoning is the most prevalent method of land use control in the United States. Usually developed and administered at the local level, the zoning ordinance typically tries to segregate land uses according to a map or plan which identifies permissible uses and intensities of development.

The notion of zoning land for agriculture has been around for a long time. Although born in the cities, zoning grew up in the suburbs, where it has been utilized to provide some semblance of order to the explosive metropolitan-area growth that began after World War II. Typically, many suburban county zoning ordinances and plans contained some kind of agricultural or open space zone, such as a minimum lot size of five acres, as a kind of "holding" area for the next ring of urban growth.

Unsurprisingly, the dynamics of suburban growth simply overwhelmed agriculture. Zoning ordinances were purportedly designed to protect farming, but the understanding between landowners, developers and governments was that when "ready" for development, special exceptions to the zoning map could be sought, and if that didn't work, the ordinance itself could be changed. Moreover, the typical ordinance made no attempt to protect farmers from the "spillover" effects of nearby urbanization. Many farmers might be able to withstand the temptation to parcel their land into five acre lots if that were the only pressure exerted on them by suburban growth. But when they pay ever-higher property taxes to provide services that they don't need to a nearby subdivision, or when nearby residents file nuisance suits against them for conducting essential farm operations, the temptation to harvest the "last cash crop"—five or ten acre ranchettes—can become all but irresistible.

If in most places the suburban model for agricultural zoning has not worked well, and was not really intended to, what about those areas where the community really is serious about protecting farmland? Is there a role for zoning there? Many local governments around the country—271 according to the National Agricultural Lands Study—are staking their agricultural future on the bet that there is not only a role for zoning, but that it will work.

And it just may, for the new breed of agricultural zoning ordinances in many instances are getting support from the farmers themselves. Says planner Robert E. Coughlin, "It is impressive that a good number of counties and municipalities have enacted such severe limitations on land use. Most of them were rock-ribbed Republican jurisdictions. The farmers supported the zoning because it protected their economic base, life style and political power. They were not enacted by urban liberals or Big City Democrats."[1]

Farmland Action In A Mid-Western County

One of those localities is Stephenson County, Illinois, in the heart of the American farm belt. West of Rockford,

Illinois, it is a land of richness in more ways than one: in soil, of course, but also in culture, aesthetics, history, and in money.

By the most common measure of urbanization pressure—population statistics—it would seem that county residents have little reason to be concerned about the impact of urbanization on their dominant industry, agriculture. In fact, throughout the 1970s, State and U.S. Census Bureau projections suggested that the county's population was in decline. The notion was disputed by local civic leaders, who could point to gains in the local workforce, and burgeoning industrial and commercial relocations in the county seat of Freeport to support their claims. And, when the preliminary 1980 Census figures came out, they turned out to be correct: the county did reverse its typical rural population loss. The 1980 population is 49,546 and growing.

But the net population gain is quite small, and by itself does not explain the significant amount of new urban development occurring within the county. Between 1968 and 1978, according to a rough estimate prepared by officials of the Stephenson County Soil and Water Conservation District, the county lost 1,000 acres of high quality agricultural land to such development each year.[2] It has occurred not only in Freeport, and in smaller towns such as Lena, Cederville and Lake Somerset, but also in unincorporated and largely rural areas. In fact, more than half of the building permits now issued are for new houses that would be located in unincorporated areas.

The pace of the new development is not necessarily inconsistent with the very modest population gain—some 700 people—shown in the 1980 Census figures. But beneath the surface of the statistics, considerable shifting around of people is probably occurring. Many of the newcomers to the county, along with long-time residents, are moving to outlying areas, and many Chicago residents—located a few hours' drive away—have purchased second homes within the county. Part-time residents are a population group not picked up by Census figures, but responsible for a good deal of direct and indirect urban growth.

Concern about the effects of agricultural land loss led Stephenson County, in 1976, to pass a highly restrictive farmland zoning ordinance which sets a 40 acre minimum lot size on Class I and II soils throughout the unincorporated areas of the county. In the unincorporated areas, these two soil classes account for 82 percent of the land.

Forty acre zoning over four-fifths of the county's rural land may seem to some as rather more governmental intervention than is warranted, but the measure has a good deal of local economic logic. Stephenson County is Illinois' leading dairy county. Feed grain production is becoming an important agricultural activity; recently, the county has attracted a multi-million dollar swine operation—the largest in Illinois—which handles 26,000 swine from suckling to slaughter.

Agriculture remains the traditional and still dominant economic activity of the county, and the growing presence of non-agricultural land uses and activity in key agricultural areas is clearly a matter of concern. Stephenson's response is intended to direct new development away from prime agricultural land, even as new growth is encouraged elsewhere.

At this point, however, the prognosis for success of this soil-based zoning system is not entirely clear—although not because of any weakening of civil resolve. The zoning should be successful in keeping most new development off Class I and Class II soils, but the interspersal of soil types within the county is so complete that there are very few farms that do not include or abut some non-prime land that is not subject to the county's 40 acre limitation. Some county officials think that development of this non-prime land will result in new residents seeking restrictions on farming. Says Del Schieder, a prominent Stephenson County farmer and planning board commissioner, "Scattered housing can ultimately destroy our farm economy, in spite of our best efforts to save it."[3]

Schieder's concern is a real one, and relates to agricultural zoning in many areas of the country. For, if Stephenson County provides a clue to the effect of rural growth in farming areas, it is that population statistics and the number of acres of prime farmland that are being converted do not provide a reliable prediction of things to come. Even with the most resolute kind of controls on "prime land," new development, even if thinly overlaid, can have permanently adverse effects for a specialized farm economy.

The difficulties which Stephenson County is experiencing in protecting their farm economy are of some moment to other areas of the heartland. The notion that the farm belt states, as well as other major farm areas, need zoning or other techniques to protect farmland has been hard to sell until recently, but is gradually catching on as new information about pressures on the resource base come to light. A 1979 survey of local soil and water conservation districts which was undertaken by the National Association of Conservation Districts found that only 5 percent of districts within the Corn Belt felt that farmland urbanization was not a problem. Observes NACD, "This region contains much of the nation's prime farmland, but also much of its industrial production, and many agricultural areas within commuting distance of industrial jobs are feeling the impact of rural growth."[4] This is borne out by regional land conversion statistics of the Department of Agriculture. Between 1967 and 1975, the Corn Belt lost more prime agricultural land to urban and water uses than any other region of the country except the Southeast, which is the fastest growing region of the country. Since the Corn Belt states have not been growing rapidly in population, the high proportion of prime land loss in the Corn Belt reflects the high proportion of high quality farmland within the region.

Other Approaches to Zoning

Stephenson's is only one approach among many — some of which have some innovative new twists.

Several Minnesota counties, for example, are utilizing what the National Agricultural Lands Study has called "fixed area-based allocation zoning," which can provide a more subtle basis for guiding growth in farm areas than either large lot zoning or simply zoning development out of prime agricultural land can provide. According to Robert Coughlin, the allocation approach is "a special case of zoning which allows a given number of dwellings on a large tract in a way that makes it possible to concentrate them in small lots in the least disruptive location on the tract."[5] In comparison with large lot zoning, this strategy makes it easier to preserve farmland in contiguous tracts.

Success with zoning seems most likely when local circumstances and conditions are kept paramount. Stephenson County may have encountered some unexpected difficulties when it chose to zone development away from prime agricultural land simply because there was so much interspersal of prime farmland and buildable lots. In other areas, prime acreage may be geographically grouped in more cohesive and contiguous units, thus more effectively segregating urban and agricultural uses.

In Black Hawk County, Iowa, for example, residential uses of certain highly productive farmland is prohibited. Black Hawk officials determine the quality of farmland through a "corn suitability rating." This approach is more sensitive as a measuring technique than the USDA's traditional soil classifications (I through VII), Black Hawkers believe. Today, 70 percent of the land in the county has a corn suitability rating of "70" or more, and is thus protected from residential development.

With few exceptions, zoning is almost wholly a local matter, and that is both a source of strength (it is close to the people) and weakness (it is easy to change, and not terribly responsive to non-local concerns). State involvement in local zoning has been highly controversial. In the late 1960s and early 1970s, there was a considerable effort made by planners and environmentalists to get state governments to assert greater control over land use decisions considered to be of more than local concern— such as siting of power plants and airports, or development of wetlands and other critically important environmental areas. Although a number of states adopted such programs, the pace of state action slackened in the mid-years of the 1970s when proposed federal assistance did not materialize.

The failure of the bulk of states to institute land regulatory programs is a reflection not only of vehement opposition to state control on the part of some landowners and local governments, but also because of the abstract and procedural orientation of proposed programs. Moreover, because agricultural land was not then considered to be in such urgent need of protection, most of the states simply ignored farmland protection in their programs. Now, with many farmers themselves concerned about urban pressures, some believe that state action to protect farmland may soon be looked on more favorably by rural areas.

"Our major message," says planner Robert Coughlin, referring to proposals for improved land use regulation, "was that the states are the key to political action."[6] The message is still apt, for it is indeed unlikely that the piecemeal activities of scattered rural governments will be adequate to protect farmland fairly and permanently unless state governments become seriously involved.

Oregon's Statewide Growth Control Program

So far, only one state government—that of Hawaii—has actually gone so far as to impose zoning directly. Because of the state's unique historical and economic circumstances, with a quite centralized form of government and a high value specialty-crop agriculture, the Hawaiian approach is not especially transferable to other states. In some mainland states, such as Wisconsin, state governments provide incentives for local zoning. In the case of New York's Adirondack Park region, the state government provides detailed guidelines and close participation in major land use decisions for this quite special, semi-wilderness area.

For a truly comprehensive effort on the part of a mainland state government to protect farmland, however, one must look to Oregon. Since 1973, Oregon has had an extensive planning program overseen by a state "Land Conservation and Development Commission" (LCDC). The LCDC program provides the basic framework for local planning, through 19 statewide guidelines. The guidelines address most planning issues ranging from air quality to housing to coastal shoreland protection that pertain to growth control. But the most visible and immediate of the LCDC functions in controlling urbanization comes about through a mandate to all towns and cities with a population of 2,500 or more to impose "urban growth boundaries," and to establish "exclusive farm use" zones.

The urban growth boundaries (UGB) are to allow for normal future expansion of the towns and cities, perhaps through 1990 or the year 2000. But the establishment of the boundaries effectively marks the limit of the extension of urban services for the foreseeable future. The stated policy objective for this action is, in most areas, to hold down the cost of offering new services by forestalling diseconomic leapfrog development and to protect agricultural land from conversion to urban use.

The "exclusive farm use" (EFU) zones are off limits to most urban development. Identified through state guidelines, but established and policed by local government, these areas are customarily at some distance from cities and are nearly entirely in farm ownership. The establishment of such zones provides benefits to the farmers themselves, as the zoning carries with it substantial property tax reductions, along with protection against local ordinances which unreasonably restrict farm practices and assurance that only compatible non-farm uses will be allowed within the zone.

This kind of state-level involvement in land use is never easy to achieve. Even in Oregon, which enjoys the reputation of being one of the most environmentally conscious of states, developing the kind of consensus needed to implement a statewide land use program has required exceptional dedication and commitment on the part of political leaders, state and local officials and citizens. The Oregon program has twice been subjected to a statewide referendum—in 1976 and 1978—and in both cases more than 60 percent of those voting supported the program. The regulations have also been subjected to a barrage of legal challenges, most of which have been resolved in favor of the LCDC, the regulatory agency.

If the process of implementing the Oregon program has been time-consuming it has been time well spent, for public support for the goals of the program appears to be solid. Now, the Oregon program is moving beyond an interim control program—during the planning phase— to full implementation of the 1973 law by local governments. Although it is too early to assess the program's permanent effect on land use, many fast-growing counties—some of them initially resistant to the state-level involvement—have adopted quite sophisticated planning and regulatory structures.

Southwest Oregon, where the American Land Forum conducted field studies on rural growth in 1979 for the Council on Environmental Quality,[7] is a case in point. Few areas within the state have been subject to such rampant growth, or have been in as much need for effective mechanisms to guide urbanization.

In the three-county area studied (Jackson, Josephine, and Douglas) population growth has been among the most rapid in the state, which is itself growing at rates well above the national average. Three quarters of the new population comes not from new births but from in-migration, as retirement-age people and a substantial number of younger people are attracted to the state because of its "livability."

The rhumb line of Southwestern Oregon's new growth is Interstate 5, with California at the bottom end of it. Californians come to look at Oregon, and an astonishing number of them, local accounts have it, decide to stay. One of these is ex-Californian Jon Deason of Jack-

son County, who admits, "I was an escapee. I took a pay
cut to move here, to live in a rural area." Now, as Commissioner of Jackson County, Deason is trying hard to
cope with the runaway growth. "Nobody is answering
the needs of growth," he says. "We have chaos." [8]

The natural attractions of the area work in combination with Oregon's reputation for environmental protection to attract newcomers. As a result, the counties to the
south that are closest to California expect no let up in
population growth for the forseeable future. Indeed, a
recent survey of California attitudes indicated that 29
percent of that state's citizens wish to leave, and that of
this group more wished to go to Oregon than to any other
place. To put this in perspective, it is helpful to know
that 29 percent of California's population is double the
population of Oregon.

The new growth has been accompanied by a high
level of land conversion. For example, the Jackson
County Planning Department estimates that between
3,600 and 4,400 acres within the county are being converted to residential use each year. According to the
Josephine County Soil and Water Conservation District,
30,000 acres of farmland within the county were converted to non-agricultural uses between 1974 and 1979,
and an additional 10,000 acres were idled or placed in
less intensive use.

Especially hard-pressed by the new development
has been the area's fruit growing industry. In and around
the 15-mile Medford-to-Ashland corridor is one of the
four prime pear-producing regions in the West. (The
others are Hood River, Oregon; Sacramento, California;
and Yakima Valley in Washington.) The pear orchards
and the agri-businesses associated with them are already
experiencing conflicts related to new growth.

Although only a small amount of land is in orchards

(about 11,000 acres in Jackson County), production from this acreage accounts for about half the total value of the county's agriculture each year. Yet land prices have increased so much ($5,000 to $7,000 per acre) that it has become prohibitive to replant many declining orchards in Medford, just as it became prohibitive to so do in San Fernando or Santa Clara counties in California two decades before. Non-farming residents complain about spraying and frost protection activities. Moreover, some once viable farm units are being split into "hobby" farms. Those with just a few trees may not care for them efficiently since their livelihood does not depend on it, thus allowing pests or diseases to gain a foothold in other orchards.

As aggregate production declines, the packing and distribution facilities which require a certain minimum input for scale economies to be realized are then threatened. When the existence of these secondary agricultural support facilities is in doubt, farmers are understandably reluctant to replant long-term crops such as orchards, and a vicious cycle is completed.

It seems clear that urban pressures left unchecked will produce major changes in the area's agriculture. Agriculture has traditionally been the number two money-maker of Jackson County's economy—behind forestry. With the new urban growth, it now ranks third.

The best hope for agriculture in the area is the growth mediating process established by the state. After a prolonged process of identifying urban and agricultural boundaries, all three counties have now submitted their programs for LCDC review. It is too early to assess how effective the "urban growth" and "exclusive farm use"approaches will be in containing new growth within pre-set boundaries. But the clear segregation of agricultural and urban uses envisioned by the plans will now be tested.

To be sure, the eight year process of putting the plans into effect has taken its toll ("it just came along ten years too late," Jackson Commissioner Deason says ruefully)[9] and yet, without the state program it is doubtful that any of the three counties would have been able to muster the political will to adopt such comprehensive measures. In fact, while some Douglas County citizens have been in opposition to the state program, the county has adopted a good program by most accounts.

Today, there is more than a little reason for optimism that the tools provided by the Oregon legislature—the alphabet soup of LCDC, UGB and EFU—is working, even under the difficult circumstances in the Southwestern part of the state. "Although farm land prices climbed in every part of the U.S. last year," says Richard P. Benner, Co-director of the 1000 Friends of Oregon, "they dropped in Oregon, suggesting improved stability in farm areas. Oregon counties, as of January 1980, have zoned 12 million acres for exclusive farm use—including 117 million acres in the growth-pressured Willamette Valley. No compensation was paid any landowner. . . And, most important, farmland protection is only one part of Oregon's growth management program. . . . The balance of the overall program allays much criticism (e.g. from homebuilders) that would otherwise plague the farmland protection efforts."[10]

By the summer of 1981, Oregon had become the clear leader among states with farmland protection programs. According to Ron Eber, a farmland specialist with the LCDC, 55 percent of all privately owned land in the state is now in an Exclusive Farm Use Zone.[11] Moreover, now that the local land use plans have been completed, the state legislature, in its 1981 session, has moved to assure continuing LCDC oversight of local changes in their plans.

4

Sharing Ownership:
Development Rights

In rapidly growing or heavily developed areas, zoning to protect farmland is often viewed as inadequate. There are a good many exceptions, of course, and some of the most effective examples of farmland zoning now going on in this country are in metropolitan areas. But these usually have involved also some degree of state or regional government oversight of local zoning. The problem with local zoning is, as a suburban planner once put it, that "the work of generations can be undone by three men in three minutes."

In areas such as the Northeast, where development pressures are so intense that creating and keeping a pro-zoning consensus for farmland is difficult, some states and localities are mounting efforts to purchase development rights to farmland. "Purchase of Development Rights"—PDR for short—involves purchasing a deeded interest in land for an amount of money equivalent to the difference between the value of the land for development and its value for agriculture.

The approach offers the advantage of permanence: once development rights have been acquired by the state or county, the landowners may continue to live on the land and use it for agriculture or other uses consistent with farming, but the owner's right to develop the land is extinguished.

The problem is the expense. Among those governments that have tried it, according to the National Agricultural Lands Study, it has cost an average of $1,800 per acre to buy up development rights to farmland. There is a kind of Catch-22 in this, for in areas where development rights would be cheap, the technique is not thought to be needed, while where it is more clearly required, development pressures are so intense that the costs of purchasing developing rights are so very high that only a small amount of acreage can be protected this way.

Nonetheless, some urbanizing communities and a few states have been willing to foot the bill—albeit on a very modest scale in so far as acreage is concerned. By the fall of 1980, they had paid out $18 million to buy up the development rights on 10,000 acres of farmland. With another $100 million authorized for PDRs in locations scattered across the Northeast and in Washington State's King County, 50,000 acres in total will be under easements soon.[1]

Such acreage is insignificant nationally, amounting to only .01 percent of the cropland base, but the PDR technique can be important locally—especially in areas where farmland preservation complements other objectives such as open space and historic preservation.

The Suffolk County Program

Suffolk County, Long Island, is an example of farmland easements serving several public purposes. When the county legislature, in 1976, approved a $21 million bond issue for a PDR program, it was clear that if something weren't done soon farming would all but disappear from the county. Since 1960, Suffolk's population had jumped from 600,000 to 1.3 million, and planners were predicting three million people by 2020. In the previous twenty years, the county's producing farm acreage had shrunk from about 100,000 acres to 40,000 acres. Yet, on this acreage the county still produced the greatest cash crop (about $100 million per year, mostly from potatoes and cauliflower) of any county in New York State.

There were other reasons, too, why the county legislature was willing to take the political risk of being among the first governments in the country to try to purchase farmland development rights. According to former County Executive John Klein, the architect of the program, the new residents—most of them clustered in the densely populated western part of the county—accepted the program because "they wanted to be able to drive through farmland, show their children potato farms, and pick strawberries in roadside fields. They didn't want to live in wall-to-wall suburbs."[2] Still, the vote was close, and when three county legislators who had voted for the bond issue were voted out by the electorate the following year, some political analysts saw a connection.

Klein himself was defeated in his bid for a third-term as County Executive, although to an opponent who supports the PDR program. His replacement, Peter Cohalan, calls the farms that have been preserved "a testimony to the agricultural history of the county."[3] There is, however, some question as to just how extensive that testimony will be.

Klein had a goal of putting 15,000 acres under easement, or about 40 percent of the county's remaining farmland. However, the initial authorization by the legislature, for which the $21 million bond issue was approved, was for only about 3200 acres of farmland. With much fanfare by the local and even national press, the land (in 50 parcels) was brought under easement in September, 1977.

Ironically, owing to a building slump in 1976 and 1977, the initial easements were negotiated at less than half the cost authorized by the legislature, but county planners were not able to capitalize on this by doubling the acreage under easement. To go beyond the 3,200 acres further authorization by the county legislature is needed and it has not been forthcoming. In fact, the slackening of development pressures has given opponents of the program time to gather new strength.

If a new round of purchases does take place, the county will have no shortage of bids from which to pick and choose. It has received offers from 640 landowners covering over 30,000 acres. But the political difficulties the program has run into may mean that county planners, anxious to avoid farm islands among the subdivisions, will have a hard time in putting together contiguous farm parcels. Even in the initial phase, only about half the land was in contiguous parcels, the rest being spread out in various political jurisdictions. The next phase, when it comes, may well involve PDRs closer to where most of the people live in the densely populated west end of the county. As an open space and political selling point that may be an advantage, but it won't do much to maintain a viable farm economy in the county.

Farmland Preservation in Maryland

Maintaining a farm economy is just what the state of Maryland is trying to do through its Agricultural Land Preservation Foundation, established by the Maryland legislature in 1977. It is a good example of how a PDR program can be combined with other techniques (in this case agricultural districting) to have an effect beyond the dollars (in this case quite modest) available for farmland preservation.[4]

For Maryland, like Wisconsin, has discovered that if

one can create a constituency for farmland preservation among landowners, county governments may be induced to support and actively implement preservation programs. Some counties don't need any prodding, of course. In fact, Howard County established its own PDR program in 1976, prior to Maryland's state-level legislation. The county—within the Baltimore-Washington urban corridor—was already one of the country's leading local proponents of farmland preservation.

As in the Wisconsin zoning program, the Maryland state program was crafted in a way that encourages landowners themselves to push for county action. For landowners to be eligible to receive money for their land it must first be in an agricultural district. In order to establish an agricultural district, the county must have a right-to-farm ordinance in effect as well as an Agricultural Preservation Advisory Board. At this point state government may assist in purchasing easements in the amount of 60 percent of the cost.

The program has generated a good bit more farmland preservation activity around the state than might be anticipated, despite an initial funding level of only $6.3 million in 1979. Within six months, all 23 Maryland counties had established agricultural preservation advisory boards. This is important, because the boards, in addition to their advisory function to county government on districts and easements, can provide a kind of institutional presence for farmland preservation. Additionally, within the first six months, 13 counties had passed right to farm ordinances, and 100 agricultural districts, involving 22,000 acres, had been formed. By the end of 1980 farmland district acreage stood at 30,000.

The figure might not seem remarkable, were it not for the fact that, unlike most state districting laws, the Maryland statute actually prohibits landowners in an agricultural district from developing their land for at least five years. Given the modest funding available, the acreage now in districts far exceeds that which is likely to be brought under easements any time soon.

Still, it's a step some landowners, even with an inclination to sell their development rights, find hard to take. "We have landowners who won't commit themselves to districts for a five year period because of lack of assurance from the state that easements will actually be purchased in that time," says Dennis A. White, who ad-

ministers Howard County's program.[5] To encourage them to take that step, the Howard County Executive is proposing that the county itself provide an incentive by making small annual payments against the easement once it is secured.

As the second county in the nation (after Suffolk) to adopt a PDR program, Howard's program now has 4,800 acres under easement (most of it purchased with state assistance.) Still, this is less than a fifth of the 20,000 acre goal suggested in 1976 by a citizen task force which played a key role in establishing the Howard County program. Some doubt that the voluntary approach the county is taking will ever fully succeed.

TDR: The Montgomery County Approach

It may be that Howard County, long the state's leader on farmland protection, will benefit from the experience of Montgomery County (adjacent to Washington) on its southern border, where the ability of Maryland's program to stimulate innovative local solutions is most apparent.

"Zone it, regulate it, TDR it, or buy it," recommended the Maryland National Capitol Park and Planning Commission to the county council, and that is just what the council is setting out to do in so far as about half the country's 140,000 acres of remaining farmland is concerned.[6] The program, approved in 1980, is intended to protect both farmland and farming, and also to help reduce urban sprawl from engulfing the 40 percent of the county that is still rural open space.

Of central importance to the county's strategy is a much talked about but little tried variant on the development rights theme—called transfer of development rights or (TDRs). The TDR approach involves the conveyance of development rights from one parcel of land to another. Unlike the PDR approach, government does not actually have to acquire the development rights, but through a kind of sleight of hand, permits the private market to accomplish this. In as concise a definition of the concept as has yet been put forth, the NALS explains: "Development rights on land in a designated preservation area may be purchased by a developer and transferred to a designated development area where the equivalent amount of additional development can be constructed."[7]

The technique has been authorized in about a dozen localities around the country, but according to NALS after 47 years of collective experience among these various locales, only five transfers (involving the preservation of a total of 184 acres and the development of 107 acres) have taken place. Part of the problem is that most TDR ordinances are voluntary on the part of the developer: as long as sufficient densities can be achieved outside of protection areas, why bother with a largely untried concept that could result in delays and possibly complicated legal proceedings?

Montgomery County thinks it may have solved that problem by combining TDRs with zoning. Basically, it works this way: On farmland slated for the most intensive preservation effort (about 74,000 acres) actual development would be limited to one house per 25 acres — the equivalent of 25 acre zoning. However, owners of such parcels could recapture part of the loss of value of their land produced by the zoning by selling the rights to develop an additional 5 dwelling units, which would then be sent or "transferred" to a "receiving" area elsewhere in the county considered appropriate for high density development.

The approach is still voluntary in the sense that no one has to sell or buy development rights to develop property within the limits of the existing zoning ordinance. But the county is backing up its farmland program with some important incentives and disincentives, including a revolving fund to kick off the TDR program, limitations on water and sewerage (provided to the farm protection area), and conversely provision of "receiving" areas (yet to be established) which would be provided a high level of urban services — including water and sewer lines — well suited for high density development. Moreover, landowners in the agricultural reserve, if they wish, can participate fully in the state's districting and easement program.

Will it work? No one is certain at this point, but the approach is well thought of in the planning community. The plan won an American Planning Association award in 1981. In theory, the Montgomery program will help protect about half the farmland left in the country, curb sprawl, and encourage denser building patterns to accommodate new growth in this large metropolitan county.

As is the case with many of the country's most admired farmland protection programs the Montgomery County approach involves the overlaying of a series of techniques—not just a single technique. And the program is geared—in much the same way as Oregon's statewide program and the Twin Cities regional program in Minnesota—toward not only protecting farmland but toward guiding new development to places that make the most sense from the perspective of public facilities and services.

5

The Politics of Preservation

"I started in 1932 alongside my father . . . and now I've got one son and a couple of grandsons in the business. We do fine, but if I sold this land and put the money in the bank, we'd make more just on interest. As the value of land grows, so does the pressure to sell. What the development rights do is let us cash in some of our chips earlier." Thus spoke Jones, a New Jersey farmer who offered to sell development rights to the state.[1]

The story is is a familiar one. Urban pressures create a growing disparity between the agricultural and development values of farmland. They create expectations on the part of all of Jones's farming colleagues — expectations which, rightly or not, are founded on the inflated value of the land. Tampering with those expectations means challenging what has been called the myth of the right of unrestricted use of the land.

But that "myth" is a political reality to public officials, and it is one of the reasons why protecting high quality farmland is something few quarrel with in the abstract, but has been difficult to accomplish in its specifics. Techniques are one thing, politics quite another.

As described earlier, the first efforts to protect farmland at the state level were taken over two decades ago,

when states began to adopt property tax policies that
afforded preferential treatment for farmland. Since then,
all but two states have established tax relief programs.
But these programs have been more successful in providing financial benefits to landowners—by no means all of
them farmers—than in actually preventing the development of much farmland. Then, as the failings of preferential tax treatment became known,[2] a few state and local
governments adopted additional farmland protection
measures. During the 1960s and early 1970s, when many
state governments began to reassert more direct control
over land use, some singled out agricultural land for
special attention. Hawaii and Oregon adopted farmland
protection policies as part of their overall state land use
programs. Other states—New York, New Jersey, Connecticut, Maryland, Wisconsin and Massachusetts
among others—adopted programs specifically to protect farmland in one way or another. In other cases,
local governments—Suffolk County, Long Island, and
Black Hawk County, Iowa, and Howard and Montgomery Counties in Maryland—have instituted their
own programs.

The Absence of Federal Assistance

These programs are representative of the 300 communities around the country that have adopted farmland protection programs in the last ten years. And this has oc-
cured despite the fact that no federal program exists to
channel federal funds to states and localities that are
interested in implementing farmland retention programs.

For some, these local actions in the absence of
federal prodding might seem to lend support to the argument that, left to their own devices, states and localities

will do just fine in dealing with a serious problem. And, in fact, NALS found that a "remarkable variety and complexity" of approaches are being experimented with around the country.

But there are huge gaps in the agricultural areas of the U.S. in so far as farmland protection is concerned. Despite all of the activity in the last decade, less than 20 million acres of existing or potential cropland is covered by a state or local program that is comprehensive enough to actually protect the land base. Twenty million acres is a sizeable amount of land to be sure, but not enough when it is recognized that rural population growth is bringing urbanization pressures to a good portion of a cropland base that measures over a half billion acres.

Especially disturbing is the fact that the major farm states are, for the most part, noticeably absent from the list of preservation innovators. Fifteen states produce 86 percent of our wheat, but only one, California, has even come close to adopting a farmland protection program. Fifteen states produce 91 percent of our corn, but only one, Wisconsin, has a farmland protection program. Fifteen states produce 92 percent of our soybeans, but none has a farmland protection program in place. Yet the major agricultural states have significant agricultural land conversion problems. The Corn Belt states lost as much prime agricultural land as any other region in the 1967-1975 period. Furthermore, because of the high proportion of prime land in these states, significant loss of prime land can be expected in the future.

Fortunately, there are some signs that the major farm areas are beginning to take the land use issue seriously, and for good reason. Where farming is as big a business as the land uses that might replace it, there is a clear public purpose in protecting the land base for agriculture—especially when such protection does not necessarily preclude other land uses, but simply requires that new uses be located more carefully. Possibly the chances for action would be greater if there were some federal assistance available to states and localities, but, as discussed earlier, such assistance has yet to be enacted by Congress. And because opponents have characterized the legislation as an effort to assert an unwanted federal government role in state and local land use decision-making process, it is unlikely that there will be much federal assistance for farmland protection in the years to come, however innocuous such legislation may be.

The Market as Allocator of Farmland

Many people are instinctively opposed to any kind of governmental intervention in land use—even local intervention—preferring instead the invisible hand of Adam Smith to the visible hand of the bureaucrat. For them, land use decisions are best left to the marketplace, with price the final arbiter among competing land uses.

Market forces have their virtues. For one thing, they require no bureaucracies. They also have their costs. For farmers to outbid developers, one would have to imagine enormously high food prices which would be inflationary across-the-board, which would reduce foreign markets substantially and thus increase the trade deficit, and which would be catastrophic for the poor in this country and abroad.

Moreover, as NALS was able to document, the land market in urbanizing areas is afflicted by what NALS calls "misinformation." Along the urban fringe, where development pressures are heavy, the prospect of future development causes far more land to be idled prematurely than the immediate—or even the long term needs—of development would call for. One recent survey of the urban fringe of four cities showed that nearly half the fringe land was either in residential use or left idle; just 18 percent of the land parcels were actually farmed. NALS believes that this inefficient process will be replicated in many of the rural areas of the country that are now experiencing population growth: "the new growth will create unrealistic expectations of development that will encourage the premature withdrawal of farmland from production."

It may be that in those increasingly few rural areas that are wholly remote from urban pressures, market forces can work reasonably well without benefit of a superimposed preservation program. For most communities, the question is not simply one of market "efficiency" in the allocation of its land resources, but whether the results of the allocation process are acceptable—economically, socially, and environmentally. Scattered growth, leapfrog development and other variants of urban sprawl create growth problems for the community. Typically, such development carries with it relatively greater air and water pollution, higher energy expenditures for transportation, and greater public and private expenditures for infrastructure and services than would be associated with development that is placed closer to preexisting settlement.

The adamant believer in the workings of the market most likely would not accept responsibility for such diseconomies. There are few instances when the market is free to work alone in allocating land. Zoning ordinances, preferential real estate taxes, the Internal Revenue Code and many other government policies can severely distort the market under certain conditions. Thus, some land which, for efficiency's sake, ought to be developed, may be encouraged to be kept off the market, while more distant land is prematurely built up. But for those who are not so ideologically oriented, the most plausible solution to such distortions is not so likely to be found in the unimpeded operation of the market place as it is in adjustments to the policies where needed. Concluded participants in USDA's 1975 Prime Lands Seminar: "The present market system is not adequate to assure protection and rational utilization of our productive land resources over the long run. Actions by local, state, and federal agencies will be essential to supplement the land market process in allocating land resources among competing uses."[3]

Who Should Act?

Unfortunately, acceptance of this proposition doesn't solve many problems; instead it raises new ones. Most particularly: Who is to take the action to "supplement the market process?" Will it be the state or the local government which will have the decisive voice in land-use decisions? And will federal encouragement be required (and if so, how much, and with what "strings") to make sure that proper decisions will be made?

There is nothing new about the power struggle between layers of government. Some states have succeeded in reasserting their authority over land use— Oregon with its "package" of land use legislation for example. Others have either failed or achieved very limited statewide authority.

Allocation of land-management responsibility and authority cannot be decided in the abstract. They have to be hammered out through the political process. But there are some fundamental questions which should be raised and answered.

Some suggest that the state government ought to

provide guidance to local communities which would, in turn, be responsible for implementing a farmland preservation program. But how much guidance? And should states have the power of veto over local plans? On the one hand, detailed guidance often fails adequately to reflect the diversity within a state. This is a complaint that states themselves often lodge against the federal government. On the other hand, overly general guidance leaves less responsible or less competent governments free to emasculate, or botch, a program.

Those who advocate exclusive local control, without interference from state government (alone or with a federal encouragement), are obliged to answer another kind of question: Can the hundreds of thousands of local decisions, taken in isolation without benefit of comprehensive goals and guidelines, effectively protect an invaluable national resource? Is there a danger that the limited perspectives of local governments may fail to recognize what may be visible only in a larger context?

"Conversion of a small portion of a community's agricultural land to nonagricultural uses," says NALS, "may lower current development costs and appear insignificant in contrast to the nation's vast endowment of agricultural resources. Yet, the effects of such conversions are cumulative, and contribute over time to significant and avoidable reductions in agricultural potential and environmental quality."[4]

Equity and the Right to Develop

And then there is the politically difficult issue concerning the cost and equity factors associated with regulation or with the acquisition of development rights.

In commenting on compensable regulation of farmland, under discussion in Oregon in the early 1970's, one state official mused: "The lawyer in me says, I'm damned if we have to pay anybody to down-zone, just so long as the landowner still has use of his land. Nobody has an inalienable right to develop. But the politician in me says, it may be wise to take the compensable zoning route."

When the Howard County, Maryland, citizen task force considered ways to save farming in its jurisdiction, it came up with some guiding principles for their plan—among them: the plan must respect the market value of the farmland, be economically viable for owners of other prime agricultural areas and not impose an unrealistic burden on taxpayers or homeowners. The plan should recognize that land is the older farmer's bank account and estate, and that the farmer's long-run as well as short term interests must be preserved. Not surprisingly, the task force recommended a development-rights purchase program, rather than zoning.

New Jersey's Blueprint Commission was inspired by similar thought: "The constitutional rights of landowners should be protected from confiscatory measures as their lands are included in an open space preserve; and they should be justly compensated for the value of property rights taken from the land."[5]

Equity for the farmer does not come cheap. A Pennsylvania official told a Congressional Subcommittee hearing: "We calculate . . . that to purchase today development rights for merely 10 percent of the prime agricultural land in Pennsylvania will cost us over $800 million." And, as he noted in his testimony, the state was struggling with a $500 million deficit at the time.

According to a recent report, a New Jersey pilot program would have had to pay $1,700 to $2,300 per acre for development rights instead of the originally estimated $1,000 per acre. The pilot program was designed to test the feasibility of purchasing development rights as a way to implement the Blueprint Commission's target, the preservation of one million acres of farmland. That the program has been abandoned is hardly surprising.

Given the temper of the times, especially the anti-public-spending mood, it seems improbable that very many urban and suburban voters are going to sanction expensive programs for saving farmland. Nor are they inclined to pay the political cost involved in reducing the farmers' land-value expectation.

The dilemma is a difficult one. How can the community satisfy the landowner's notion of equity and still keep the cost at politically acceptable levels?

Safeguarding Farming

Perhaps part of the problem is that communities (and indeed the state and federal government) have been slow to recognize that "equity" to a farmer can mean far more than just property rights. When the USDA held meetings around the country for *A Time to Choose*—its Structure of Agriculture Study—Phyllis Rambo, a farmer and a grandmother from Frankfort, Kentucky, was asked by former Secretary of Agriculture Bob Bergland why she stayed with farming. Mrs. Rambo responded: "Well, we stayed with farming because we like farming. We like the ground. We like the dirt. We like to see things grow. Then, we're our own boss. We can quit in the middle of the day, if we want to, and it's a good and free life. It's working hand-in-hand with our maker."[6]

Unfortunately, one of the drawbacks to many of the existing local programs designed to safeguard farmland from conversion to nonagricultural use is that they do not ensure the continuation of farming. Maintaining a viable farm economy depends, in large measure, on profitability, and profitability is, in turn, affected by a host of factors unrelated to land. As an official from Connecticut warned: "There isn't much point in preserving our valuable agricultural acres if, for economic reasons, our farmers cannot survive and are forced to sell out. This is happening at an increasingly alarming rate in Connecticut."

Urban planners have long been preoccupied with the preservation of open space. On their multicolored maps, however, the green of the golf course is no different from the green of a farm. Moreover, on their maps—and on visual inspection—ten 100-acre farms produce roughly the same amount of open space as a single 1,000-acre farm. But are the economic prospects of the large and small farm the same?

Not in the light of what is happening in many parts of the country, as documented by *A Time To Choose* and other recent reports by USDA, for the farm economy is changing. In 1959, the average size of a U.S. farm was 288 acres; in 1978, it was over 400 acres. In 1959, there were 4.1 million farms; in 1978, the number was down to 2.67 million. Of the total "land in farms", nearly 30 percent was in the hands of about just 64,000 owners in 1978.

Since 1959, the percentage of all tracts purchased which went toward farm enlargement as opposed to establishment of new farms has more than doubled—from 29 to 63 percent in 1976, dropping to 58 percent in 1977. USDA believes that the process is unlikely to slow down, basing its forecast on the continued increase in average horsepower per tractor and the increased management capabilities associated with higher levels of education.

In 1976, according to USDA, "35 percent of farmland purchases were made by local nonfarmers, noncounty residents, or 'other'." In New Jersey, it is reported that one of the difficulties encountered in implementing the pilot development rights project was in assembling large contiguous agricultural preserves. The explanation: "So much of the land was owned by real estate brokers, land speculators and nonfarming corporations, all of whom bought the land primarily for its speculative or development value."

The Howard County task force found that virtually no farms had been bought in recent years because land prices had risen too much. One out of every three acres farmed in the county was on rented land, making leasing essential to farming. Nationally, in 1974, there were 905.6 million acres in farms. Some 367.7 million acres were rented.

These are just some of the trends that the USDA's *A Time to Choose* assessed. In brief, its overall purpose was to investigate the various circumstances and conditions—size of farms, landownership, management factors, responsiveness to change, and other characteristics of the industry of agriculture. It was able to document as never before that federal farm policies have played a major role in encouraging the trend toward increasing domination of the market by larger farm units. Among its general conclusions: current tax policies tend to favor the large landowner and wealthy investors; technology (much of it subsidized by federal R & D) and the marketing system are oriented to serve the larger producers; and commodity and credit policies have also provided greater benefits to larger producers.

As to whether these trends should be encouraged, the study argues against the notion that it is desirable for farms to become larger because they are more efficient: ". . . it has become increasingly evident that the gains to the nation that remain to be captured from the continued shift to larger and larger farming operations have become smaller over time. When the net losses to the farming communities associated with the continual decline in the number of farm families is taken into account, we have passed the point where any net gain to society can be claimed from policies that encourage large farms to become larger."[7]

In fact, as a general rule, most of the economies derived from size can be achieved on a quite small farm. Thus, for example, a wheat-barley farm in the Northern Plains that is just 175 acres in size would attain 90 percent of the economies of a 1,475 acre farm—the point where 100 percent economies are achieved. In the average of six different situations investigated by USDA, the 90 percent level of possible economies was achieved when farm size was 314 acres (with sales of $45,000) while the 100 percent level required a farm size of 1,157 acres, and sales of $133,000. The study concludes: ". . . there is no overall reason for public policy to encourage farm growth and consolidation beyond the size necessary to be efficient. Beyond this size, society has no reason to subsidize growth, nothing to gain either in terms of efficiency or lower food costs, and little to gain in terms of ensuring adequate incomes for farmers."[8]

Farming Structure and Land Use

The land use implications of increasing domination of the market by larger farm units, the increasing difficulty confronting the small farmers, the dependence on rented land, and the growing number of absentee owners whose longer-range interests are in doubt were summed up by former Secretary Bergland in his introduction to *A Time To Choose*. "The success of our agriculture is true," Bergland writes, "but it is also true that, by 1978, about 7.7 percent of the households in America owned all the farm and ranch lands. Of those households, 62,260—the population of a medium sized city—owned three of every ten acres. How did this come about in a nation that came into being with one of its principles being the widespread ownership of property? Ownership of property is still one of Americans' most cherished dreams, but this was dramatic evidence that few were achieving it, if their dream involved farmland. What is more, about 70 percent of those who owned farmland in 1978 were over 50 years old. That land will be changing hands in the next 20 or 30 years, so now is the time when we should be thinking hard about the direction in which we want to go."[9]

Bergland's observations—and indeed the structure study taken as a whole—raise some provocative questions for those interested in farmland preservation, for it may be that the urbanization issue and the "family farm" issue are elements of a single, albeit multifaceted, problem. Farming and farmland are not really separable and the "politics of preservation," which ultimately must win the support of a sizeable fraction of farmers to succeed, probably will not improve until this is understood.

Indeed, the loss of rural land to urbanization, even at a three-million-acre rate, is a curiously abstract problem when taken by itself. What's required is a fuller understanding of the "linkages"—the implications and consequences of this loss—in wholly concrete and human terms. Productivity and farm income, higher consumer prices, foreign trade and national security—these are the issues implied by a shrinking land base.

But even these are somewhat rarified. The farmland protection issue will be given greater concreteness—and consequently political clout—if it can be connected with the range of issues having to do with the simple right to own land and farm it; with the viability of small proprietorships as the backbone of American agriculture; with the conservation of the richest soils ever given to any nation.

That they are related can scarcely be doubted in a country that has lost over 88 million acres from "land in farms" in less than a decade. Those who might look for the political significance of this decline might very well find it in the sudden emergence of the "right to farm" movement. Unheard of a few years ago, over 16 states since 1979 have adopted laws intended to protect farmers when conflicts with urbanization arise. Yet these statutes do little to address the basic causes of impermanence and instability that make it so difficult for the small landowner to continue farming.

As for soil and water conservation, current agricultural practice, with its emphasis on ever increased production, has tended to undermine many of the conservation gains that were begun in the 1930s. This is not entirely a matter simply of large farms versus small farms, but a question of whether the ethic of stewardship itself is in danger. For example, while the ever increasing size of farm machinery has made many conservation practices installed in previous decades obsolete, there has not been widespread adoption of newer conservation practices more in keeping with today's needs. Urban pressures, too, play their role: farmers whose expectations for their land involve development in a decade or so are reluctant to invest in conservation systems, and may conduct their operations with less concern about the long term integrity of the soil. The most recent USDA estimate is that more than 140 million acres of crop land are eroding at levels beyond the capacity of natural processes to replenish the soil.

The fact that federal programs themselves have had a great deal to do with the centralizing trend in farm

structure, with current difficulties in soil and water conservation, and with the decentralization of urban growth
to rural America, may provide an opportunity to explore
new ways to integrate issues that have not been integrated before. Because of insistent problems concerning
land ownership, energy, agricultural "structure," resource allocation, and a host of other concerns, farm
policy is probably in for a major sorting-out during the
decade of the 1980s. With a larger framework for debate,
the Congress might be able to see the issue of farmland
protection as an important goal that can help comprehensively to insure the overall viability of U.S. agriculture—
not, as some seem to think, a subversive effort to impose
national land use planning.

To some, it might appear that the 1980 election returns mean that the proponents of legislation essaying to
protect the land base have been put more or less permanently to rout. Certainly, with a new administration that
has adamantly opposed the federal government's protec-
tive stance towards even its own land and a more conservative Congress than the one that rejected Congressman
Jeffords farmland preservation bill, the likelihood of a
major new federal program is all but ruled out. Yet the
cropland issue itself transcends party lines and political
ideologies.

President Reagan's Secretary of Agriculture John
Block, in his early pronouncements on the subject,
sounded very little different than President Carter's
Agriculture Secretary Bergland. Calling farmland conversion a "potential crisis on several counts," Block lent
his support to implementing the recommendations of the
NALS.

Given the magnitude of the problem, those recommendations, in so far as the federal government is concerned, are fully in keeping with the Republican concept

of federalism. The recommendations are for a Presidential or Congressional articulation of the national interest in agricultural lands in order to signal their importance. They ask the federal government to find ways to minimize the impact of federal and federally supported activities and policies that directly or indirectly encourage the conversion of prime agricultural land. (So far, only USDA and EPA have done so.) They call on the USDA to expand its technical assistance and education capabilities in order to help states and localities establish farmland protection programs, as well as to establish an Agricultural Land Information Center. And, as for financial assistance, they call for consideration of small matching grants to help states and localities develop programs as well as a re-imbursable agricultural land resource fund which would be self-sustaining once started. This emphasis on state and local action, encouraged by federal support but stopping far short of federal intervention, is clearly consistent not only with what most proponents of farmland preservation have been saying all along, but also with the political tenor of the times.

Part II

Beyond Open Space

Farmland as a Strategic Resource

6

The Global Context

The 1980s are not the first time that farmland preservation has been a key item in the agenda of the conservationists. In the massive building boom that followed World War II there was much concern when farmland on the edge of large cities stopped producing vegetables or corn, and began growing another cash-crop—suburban tract housing. "Low-grade urban tissue," Lewis Mumford called it, and a generation of city planners took suburban sprawl as their own particular *bete noir.*

Farmland figured prominently in their plans to preserve open space and to avoid some of the costs involved in building infrastructure, but not because this land was thought to be important to agriculture. Open space—not agriculture—was what was at issue. Moreover, if postwar planners and conservationists worried about the loss of farmland, it was greeted with scarcely concealed glee by the farmers themselves. "Scratch a farmer," said one practitioner of the art in Oregon's Willamette Valley, "and you'll find a subdivider." In Minnesota at the edge of the Twin Cities, another farmer said, "Why a man'd be a fool not to sell out at $2,000 per acre."

Indeed, in view of the extraordinary crop surpluses that characterized U.S. agriculture in the 1950s and

1960s, there was little reason to become alarmed about the U.S. farmland base. Loss of open space and urban sprawl aside, urban land uses accounted for only a tiny fraction of America's 1.3 billion acres of privately-owned farmland. With between 30 and 50 million acres of idle land immediately available for planting and an additional 266 million acres thought to be in "ready reserve" for crop production if needed, the U.S. had more than enough cropland for any conceivable contingency. Or so it seemed at the time.

First, the Good News

In fact, despite occasional setbacks, post-depression agriculture in the U.S. and, indeed, worldwide was one of the good news items in a century during which massive population dislocation from field to factory, world wars, atomic horrors, and other troublesome aspects of global industrialization preoccupied parliaments and palaces.

In even the most rigorous terms of productivity—yield per acre cultivated—the trend lines seemed bound ever-upwards. Advances in irrigation, fertilization, pest control, and mechanization permitted the achievement of greater yields at greater cost efficiency, and promised even more. As a result, farmers could produce more and more on less and less land. To keep farm prices up, production had to be restrained. The U.S. was not alone in curbing production, either. Canada and Australia were doing the same.

These trends were by no means limited to the United States and other affluent countries. By the late 1960s, as the Green Revolution began to take effect, food production in most of the less developed regions of the world was keeping ahead of population growth. Agricultural analysts looking at the statistics of production could (and did) predict that hunger soon would be eliminated if developing nations could just keep their populations within bounds.

And yet, just as doubts as to the efficacy of the Green Revolution, birth control programs, and the infusion of large amounts of capital into mechanized agricultural operations were beginning to be stilled, a series of events took place almost simultaneously in 1973 and 1974 which lacerated the complacency of all but the most pollyannish of agricultural analysts.

Among the headlines at the time: a couple of bad weather years in a row, the Russian "wheat deal," the energy crisis, and starvation in the Sahel. These matters, among others, caused reassessment of U.S. and worldwide long-range agricultural prospects, and prompted seemingly endless strategic contingency analyses relating agriculture to domestic and foreign policy — including one by the CIA itself. Instead of optimism reigning supreme, pessimism quickly became the mode, so endlessly pessimistic in fact that it became fashionably revisionist to assert that things on the farm front were not so bad as they seemed.

Today, U.S. farmers routinely produce more food than they ever have in history, but surplus grain no longer rots in rusting Liberty Ships riding at anchor in the Hudson River, and little or no land is idled deliberately. Now, agricultural specialists express perplexity when they extend current trends into the future, for the lines suggest that in a matter of a decade or so the limits of the land may be reached.

The reason for this, of course, is the vast expansion in the export market for U.S. food. Sluggish during the '50s and '60s, the market began to take off in the early 1970s, and shows no signs of abating.

"The post World War II era of chronic surpluses is over," said the U.S. Department of Agriculture in *A Time to Choose*, adding: "The decision in 1971 to let the dollar float in foreign exchange markets effectively lowered the price of U.S. products at precisely the same time foreign demand increased dramatically due to a combination of global economic, demographic, policy and weather factors."[1]

Those factors precipitated the "food crisis" of 1974—brought on not only by failure of crops in other countries, but by bad weather in the U.S. In 1972, wheat stocks in the U.S. amounted to 983 million bushels. Two years later, they had dropped to 340 million bushels. Corn stocks fell from 1.1 billion bushels to 483 million bushels. The low level of reserves was a source of worry to some, but they allowed a free-market oriented Secretary of Agriculture to proclaim the end of restrictions on production.

The result for the land base was immediate and far-reaching. During the 1960s and first year or so of the 1970s, land actually planted for principal crops each year hovered around 300 million acres, of which as little as 280 million acres was actually harvested. By 1980, farmers planted 358 million acres (not including cultivated summer fallow) and harvested 346 million.[2] They did this by putting idle land back to work, or actually expanding their cropland base by bringing new land—some of it marginal in quality—into production.

The Growth in Export Markets

Almost all of this increase was to meet export demand. In the '60s, U.S. farmers grew crops for export on about one out of every five acres harvested. Today, despite the larger base from which the figure is derived, one out of every three acres harvested is used to meet export demand.

There has been a price to pay for this much fuller utilization of cropland in terms of erosion rates that now exceed even those of the Dust Bowl. But there is no doubt that agricultural exports have become an indispensable item in the country's balance of trade, helping to offset U.S. trade deficits incurred because of oil imports, and guarding against runaway devaluation of the dollar.

Despite the urgent need of literally hundreds of millions of hungry people around the world, those who get our food, by and large, are paying for it in hard cash. "It was not physiological demand that sent up grain prices," says Philip M. Raup, a professor of agricultural economics at the University of Minnesota, "nor is it likely to be in the future. It was effective demand by people who appeared in the market place with money."[3]

Judging from the ever-increasing size of the agricultural component of our exports, this "effective demand" represents a great deal of money. After increasing slowly in the 1950s and 1960s, food export income suddenly doubled in the 1970s, then doubled again—a circumstance that has led to a characterization of the U.S. as "the OPEC of soil." In 1979, according to the National Agricultural Lands Study, "The market value of U.S. agricultural exports reached a record of $40.5 billion— $8 billion over the previous year. . . Agricultural exports now account for about 25 percent of the gross value of agricultural products sold in America and comprise nearly 20 percent of total value of U.S. exports from all sectors of the economy." Last year (1980) was the eleventh straight year in a row that exports broke the previous high record, and this occurred despite the embargo on grain to the Soviet Union which was then in effect.

The end is nowhere in sight. Most everyone expects agricultural exports to grow rapidly for the foreseeable future—although the rate of increase (the volume of agricultural exports more than doubled in the 1970s) may soon begin to slow. The National Agricultural Lands Study, in an effort to identify the likely range of export demand growth, projected that agricultural exports in the year 2000 could be as little as 390 million tons, or as much as 575 million tons, in comparison with 164 million tons exported in 1980. The mid-range projection, considered most probable by NALS, "shows that the volume of export demand will nearly triple over the next two decades, assuming constant real prices."[4] This, coupled with increased domestic demand, would require a 60 to 85 percent increase in overall agricultural production by the year 2000.

The projections are admittedly guesswork, based on assumptions about how rapidly world and U.S. population will grow, how successful other countries will be in producing their own food, and whether income growth in countries that import our food will be adequate for them to afford increasing prices. Over 70 percent of our agricultural exports are used to fatten livestock for the red meat rich diet which consumers in affluent countries are increasingly demanding. If per capita income does not grow sufficiently, these consumers may reduce their consumption of animal protein, and thus reduce demand for U.S. food. Purchasing power in middle income countries, more often used to buy staples such as wheat and rice, may also not grow as quickly as anticipated. Even so, continued growth in exports seems likely.

Hunger

For the world's poor, the increased demand for U.S. food from affluent countries means that the lowest income countries will face, in the words of *A Time to Choose,* "an ever more serious gap between the amount of food needed to meet basic human requirements and the amount they can pay for . . . in the market."[5] World food aid and technical assistance programs have helped, but are far below the level needed by the literally hundreds of millions of people who live close to the edge of starvation. "It is easy to give food aid to the needy when huge surpluses are filling domestic warehouses," say economists Sandra S. Batie and Robert G. Healy. "But in years of short harvests, food aid may come at the cost of higher prices for the U.S. consumers."[6]

In fact, the Presidential Commission on World Hunger reported to President Carter in 1980 that the U.S. contributions to world food aid and development assistance have fallen off sharply as a percentage of gross national product since the end of the 1950s. Today, 12 other donor nations devote a greater percentage of their GNP to food assistance than the U.S. Moreover, these countries are more likely than the United States to provide aid in the form of grants, rather than as a loan which must be repaid. The Commission concluded that current U.S. policies fail to reflect "America's moral, economic and national security interests in ending world hunger, nor the country's genuine concern for hungry people."[7]

Tragically, the struggle by the world's poor to increase their food supplies has, in many areas, led to serious or even irreparable damage to the soil. As populations grow beyond the limits of arable lands, the poor often migrate (or are dispossessed) to less fertile land that is more susceptible to degradation.

In many areas, the result has been the widespread loss of tropical forest—either because of overutilization of firewood, or clearing of the forest for agriculture. Where population pressures are greatest, the overwhelming immediate needs of impoverished people prevent them from utilizing agricultural or wood gathering practices that would safeguard the productivity of the land. Land tenure arrangements, under which large landowners keep the best land for themselves, have compounded the tragedy by forcing the poor to marginal land. The deforestation problem is also compounded by industrial logging, sometimes by large multi-national corporations, without adequate attention to reforestation.

According to a federal task force on deforestation, between 10 and 12 million hectares of tropical forest are denuded each year.[8] Under a "worst case" scenario, as much as half the remaining tropical forest could be lost by the turn of the century. Although the task force felt that the worst case was unlikely to occur, millions of people around the world in any case are threatened by the possible loss of wood for fuel and shelter.

Another crucial problem is desertification, the process by which arid or semi-arid land is degraded to infertile desert or desert-like conditions. According to the report of a U.N. conference on the subject, held in Nairobi in 1977, four percent of the world's population live in dry lands potentially subject to desertification. The most conspicuous example of desertification is, of course, along the southern edge of the Sahara, where 251,000 square miles of once productive land are now desert. But the problem is not limited to the Sahara. Desertification has and still is occurring in most arid and semi-arid areas in the world, including large portions of the western United States, where the pressures of population growth and overuse of soil and water resources by agriculture have brought severe desertification to 225 million acres.

According to the Presidential Commission on World Hunger, at least 800 million people in the world today are unable to afford even a minimally adequate diet. By the year 2000, world population is projected to increase from 4.2 billion people to at least 6 billion; today, three billion people (three-fourths of the world's population) live in developing countries; by 2000, the figure will be eight out of every ten people.

Food Aid Policy

Since the 1974 World Food Conference recognition has grown that food aid in and of itself is not the solution to world hunger. Rather, the solution will depend on whether the developing nations will be able to increase their own production of food to meet the needs of their growing populations. Thus, emphasis is being given to coupling of food aid to agricultural development in recipient nations; 1977 amendments to the U.S. food aid program, for example, would forgive food aid loans to recipient nations that use the food (or proceeds from its sale) for development projects that would not otherwise be undertaken.

In the end, agricultural assistance programs are only partially humanitarian in nature; they have major economic, political and strategic implications. Several countries that were formerly recipients of U.S. food aid are now good commercial customers of the United States.

Stresses the Presidential Commission on World Hunger: ". . . two straight years of bad harvests in any of the major grain-producing nations of the world could precipitate another global food crisis like the one that occurred in 1972-1974. Recurrent crises of this nature could bring widespread famine and political disorder to the developing countries and would severely disrupt a fragile world economy already weakened by energy shortages and rampant inflation. U.S. policies will have a major role in determining whether this scenario will be played out." Even now, as this is being written, the United Nations Food and Agriculture Organization reportedly is calling the world food situation "as fragile as it has been at any time since the food crisis of 1973-1974."[9] For two years in a row, the peoples of the world have consumed more grain than they have produced, and world cereal reserves are declining to the minimal levels that FAO believes safe. A good world harvest in 1981 is seen as the only hope for averting another food crisis.

Whether an immediate crisis will develop or our food aid policies change remains to be seen. But it is not the lowest-income countries that are most dependent on U.S. food, even though they need it most. Rather, it is countries like Japan, the Soviet Union, West Germany, Britain, and Saudi Arabia that have provided the push that has brought the U.S. to the position of being the world's preeminent supplier of food. "In the early 1950s," warns the USDA's *A Time to Choose,* "the rest of the world depended upon the U.S. for 2 percent of its agricultural supplies; by the late 1970s, it depended on the United States for 11 percent. . . By 1985, the rest of the world could well be buying 15 percent of its food, feed and fiber supplies from the United States."

7

Is There Land Enough?

Behind the huge surge in world food demand, and the
various projections of that demand into the future, lies a
more elusive question: what of the effect on American
farmland? Of the 2.3 billion acres in the United States,
about 1.3 billion is privately owned agricultural land.
About 413 million acres are regularly used for crop production, and another 127 million acres are considered to
have a high or medium potential for conversion into crop
production if the need arises—for a total cropland resource pool of 540 million acres. Most of the remaining
800 million acres may be useful for range, forests or
pasture—but is considered to have a low or zero potential to be used economically for crop production.

For all practical purposes, it is the 413 million acres
now in existing cropland plus the 127 million acres that
might be brought into production if the need arose, that
is the focus of concern about the conversion of farmland
to other uses. This is the land that the National Agricultural Lands Study believes will be at or near full utilization by the year 2000—meaning that within a score of
years, U.S. cropland reserves will be exhausted.

The NALS arrived at this by calculating how much
land it would take to meet a "most probable" demand

projection for the year 2000 under three different assumptions about future crop yields. On the one hand, if the annual growth in yields between now and the year 2000 were equal to the very high rate of increase that occurred in the 1960s, the country would need only an additional 77 million acres planted in principal crops to meet the projected level of demand. If, on the other hand, yields grew at the much slower rate that they did during the 1970s, as much as an additional 113 million acres would be needed. If yield increases were at the mid point between the rate of the 1960s and that of the 1970s, some 95 million additional acres would be needed. On the basis of these projections, NALS concluded: "by the year 2000, most if not all of the nation's 540 million acre cropland base is likely to be in cultivation. When seen from this perspective, continuing *non*-agricultural demands upon the agricultural land base become a matter for national concern." [1]

Even without the pressures of urbanization cutting into the overall size of the cropland pool, there is little certainty whether expansion of land in cultivation could be accommodated on the available land base without seriously affecting other agricultural uses. Most of the 60 million acre expansion in principal crops during the 1970s was previously land in rotational hay or improved pasture. Says the NALS Executive Director Robert Gray, "We really can't draw too much more from rotational hay and pasture land if we want to maintain the domestic livestock herd. We do have a continuing need for milk and beef, and we simply can't plow up all the pasture land in New York and Pennsylvania and Wisconsin and Minnesota to grow corn and soybeans for export while keeping stable supplies of other livestock-based products." [2]

With over 85 percent of the existing cropland base

(413 million acres) now under cultivation for principal crops alone, there is virtually no slack, since some land is not planted each year because of adverse weather, illness, and probate, and the rest is likely to be summer fallow, rotational hay or improved pasture. That leaves the 127 million acres of potential cropland on which to expand cultivation. Based on such factors as commodity prices in 1976, development and production costs, and physical soil characteristics, NALS believes that 36 million acres of this land has a high potential to be brought into crop production, while the remaining 91 million acres has only a medium potential. Says Gray: "One of the key unknowns is how much of the 127 million acres can come in and be profitably farmed without very significant real increases in commodity prices, or before rising real food prices choke back demand and reduce pressures to expand cultivated acreage. No one has the answer."[3]

It is within this context of uncertainty that the effects of a continuation of current rates of agricultural land conversion needs to be viewed. Land in the cropland resource pool is not just good land for agriculture, it is also well suited for development—i.e., it is generally flat, treeless (in the case of existing cropland), well drained, and often served by public infrastructure, the roads, water lines, and other facilities that encourage urban development.

The Data Debate and the Impermanence Syndrome

Ever since 1975, when the Soil Conservation Service conducted its "Potential Cropland Study," a seemingly endless argument has been going on among different agencies within USDA about how much cropland is converted each year to urban and built up uses that preclude agriculture. The SCS study, based on field observations, found that between 1967 and 1975 about 24 million acres of rural land—roughly a third of it cropland— was converted to urban or water uses. This rate of conversion (an average of three million acres per year) was roughly three times the rate previously thought to be occurring.

A subsequent SCS study, the 1977 "National Resource Inventories," did not assess rates of conversion, but confirmed that a far greater amount of land was devoted to urban and built-up uses than had been suspected.

This was not entirely persuasive to many USDA economists, who could point to another set of USDA statistics, developed not from field observation but data provided by Commerce Department's Bureau of the Census, which held that only 750,000 acres of land was urbanized each year, of which perhaps 250,000 to 300,000 acres came from cropland.[4]

By the time NALS was established in 1979, one could get a totally different conception of how much land was urbanized each year depending upon whom one talked to within USDA. Although NALS had neither the time nor the money to conduct its own inventory, it did sift through the various data sources, and in the end chose to rely on the SCS data as its principal source of information about the agricultural land base and conversion pressures. Thus, according to NALS, about three million acres of agricultural land (a figure that includes pasture, range and forested land) really *is* being converted to non-agricultural uses each year. Of this some 675,000 acres is taken directly from the existing cropland base, plus an indeterminate amount from the "potential" cropland base. Unfortunately, NALS was not able to determine this latter figure, nor did it provide an estimate. But the estimate widely accepted by analysts is that the total amount of land converted from current and potential cropland each year is about one million acres.

Whether this estimate is high or low is probably beside the point, despite occasionally vitriolic arguments among researchers. There is a significant danger that narrowly interpreting national statistics on the loss of cropland can greatly mislead the general public as well as policy analysts. "The acres involved," says the National Association of Conservation District's Neil Sampson, "are not large when compared with a very large resource base. But to the extent that development patterns affect the ability of neighboring farmers to do their thing without conflict, it has an effect on agricultural production itself." [5]

What Sampson is referring to is something that has come to be called the "impermanence syndrome." Urbanization does not just reduce the cropland base by displacement. Rural areas destined for future development often begin to lose a favorable environment for farming long before the actual subdivisions appear. By the time significant development comes along, the character of the farm economy may have already been radically and permanently disrupted.

The process works this way: First, land prices increase as speculators begin to recognize the development potential of an area. Then farmers, well aware of what is happening, become reluctant to invest in major, long term improvements for their farms. This, in turn, may adversely affect the local farm support industries, which may be forced to relocate or go out of business. By the time early, scattered subdivisions appear, the local agricultural infrastructure may have already been severely weakened.

Once subdivisions become established, what NALS

calls a "unique tension between those people who want to farm and those who want the land for housing or for other intensive uses" is likely to surface. Farmers can look forward to vandalism, "nuisance" lawsuits and local ordinances which restrict or even ban normal farming practices, higher property taxes, and a general decline in political power. And the new residents will have their fair share of complaints: odors from animal wastes, lumbering farm machinery slowing the long commute home, or noisily beating the alarm clock to the punch of an early morn. More serious are the potential health hazards stemming from the use of pesticides and other farm chemicals.

The feeling of impermanence is compounded by the fact that the land market in developing areas often creates false expectations on the part of landowners about the development value of their land. In urban fringe areas, NALS found that "misinformation" or uncertainty about future land needs for housing and other development affects "far more land than can reasonably be developed efficiently."[6] As a result the syndrome is aggravated by premature idling of agricultural land which produces noncontiguous or leapfrogging subdivisions, deterioration of agricultural services and a loss of community coherence.

So far, even though no one has been able to come up with a way to quantify in a comprehensive way the "spillover effects" of land development, enough pieces of information do exist to suggest that the effects can be a great deal more damaging to agriculture than the number of acres of land that are physically converted may superficially imply. According to the Soil Conservation Service's *Potential Cropland Study,* more than 24 million acres of land was being held for "future urban use" as of 1975. Half of this land was of good quality, but underutilized for agriculture because it had been isolated by zig-zag urban growth, zoned for future development or otherwise made uneconomic to crop. This has led to an unsettling, if not very precise, rule of thumb that for every acre urbanized, another acre is, for all practical purposes, lost to agriculture.

As for agricultural land in general, NALS, using the figures developed in the National Resource Inventories, believes that in addition to the three million acres of agricultural land that is directly converted to housing and other built up uses each year, a net of 2.6 million is shifted into speculative or pre-development uses. The total, five and a half million acres *per year,* thus begins to sound substantial.[7]

This figure, too, was greeted with considerable skepticism by other agencies within the Department of Agriculture—at least until the revisions were made in the 1978 Census of Agriculture recordation of changes in "land in farms." Despite the clear evidence of urbanization, the 1978 Census seemed to show a 13 million acre *increase* in the "land in farms" category between 1974 and 1978. Although not directly a measure of land conversion, the published "land in farms" data seemed wholly inconsistent with the magnitude of development pressures that SCS and NALS claimed were occurring.

As it turned out, the Census was wrong. Shortly before the completion of its study, NALS became aware that the Illinois Department of Agriculture, then headed by current U.S. Agriculture Secretary John Block, had requested the Census Bureau to clarify its 1978 Illinois Census data, which indicated that land in farms had increased within the state since 1974. The Bureau explained that the 1974 and 1969 Censuses had underenumerated land in farms. After adjustment for the underenumeration it was found that instead of a 639,000

acre increase, Illinois' "land in farms" had actually declined 425,000 acres.[8]

Building on this finding, NALS discovered that the
underenumeration was nationwide, owing to the fact that
definitions used in 1969 and 1974 differed from those in
1978. When adjustments were made for the entire nation,
it became apparent that, between 1969 and 1978, land in
farms decreased by some 88 million acres—an astonishing 9.8 million acres per year. The Census does not provide any information that would help determine what is
happening to the 9.8 million acres a year that drop out of
the "land in farms" category. Obviously, some is developed, some is idled by speculation, some parcelled for
ranchettes, and some simply may not be reported. But
the sheer magnitude of the shift was startling even to
those who tended to disbelieve the National Resource
Inventory findings. "What the availability of the adjusted
census data really showed," says Gray, "is that the conversion trend line of the NRI was accurate, or perhaps
even too low."[9]

In the past, the "impermanance syndrome" was
limited largely to the expanding fringes of the major
metropolitan areas. While it inevitably caused radical
transition in the local farm economy, and created difficult urban growth problems, its overall effect on "heartland" farming was probably minimal.

With the decentralizing trend towards rural and
small town population growth in all regions of the country, and regional population shifts to the South and West,
as well as continuing suburban growth, the total amount
of rural land potentially subject to urban land uses is
rapidly increasing.

In order to get an idea of the magnitude of this part
of the problem, NALS looked at development patterns in
the 100 counties that had the highest level of sales of

agricultural products from the farm in the nation. Between 1970 and 1978, these counties—only one third of which were metropolitan—gained population at twice the rate of the nation as a whole. In a few cases, there was a separation between the farming areas of the county and the important urban growth areas. But, in most cases, according to NALS, "the two are not separated and the population is concentrated in the farming area in a manner that makes expansion automatically encroach on farms."

Suspicion might arise that the spillover effects of urbanization may be limited largely to the major metropolitan areas, and their adjacent counties. These counties, after all, still experience the most population growth in absolute terms, and this must be accommodated on a relatively small amount of land. "The point to be emphasized here," says the NALS, "is that the rural conversion process is inherently no different than the conversion process around metropolitan areas. As population pressures continue in rural areas, productive agricultural land is likely to be prematurely withdrawn from production in response to unrealistic expectations of future development." [10]

The price of farmland—whether for agriculture or development—has been increasing rapidly—a circumstance which further destabilizes farm areas already "impermanent" or on the verge of it. Since 1970, the price of farmland has increased at two-and-one-half times the rate of inflation. In 1970 the average price per acre was $196—an average made up of areas ranging from the "garden state" prices of New Jersey at over a thousand dollars to some arid areas of the West where farmland could still be bought for less than fifty dollars an acre. But by 1980, farmland was fetching a U.S. average of $640 per acre—including $2400 in New Jersey.

According to John F. Jones of the USDA, farm real estate prices more than doubled in 12 states between 1975 and 1980—Ohio, Indiana, Illinois, Iowa, Missouri, Kentucky, Wisconsin, South Dakota, Delaware, Maryland, and Colorado. And seven states had increases of more than 20 percent as recently as 1979, with California up 20 percent, Maryland up 25 percent.[11]

As urbanization drives ever deeper into the agricultural hinterland, the gap between land prices and the value of the land for agriculture widens. And the impermanence syndrome will obviously deepen.

Erosion and the Land Base

If conversion of agricultural land to urban uses were the only farmland problem the country faced, it might seem problem enough. But the pressures from within agriculture to increase production are also taking their toll on the country's agricultural land.

More than a century ago, George Perkins Marsh, the "father" of modern conservation warned that "the future operations of rural husbandry . . . in districts yet remaining substantially in their native condition, should be so conducted as to prevent the widespread mischiefs which have been elsewhere produced by thoughtless or wanton destruction."[12]

The prophet may have been honored, but his advice was not, and the mischiefs showed up, spectacularly, in the dustbowl '30s. Despite Marsh's belief that the ownership of the land by those who tilled it would produce a husbandry of long-range stewardship, by the time 1940 rolled around some 100 million acres had been damaged, much of it irreversibly, in less than a decade. "I can lime it, crossplough it, manure it, and treat it with every art known to science," President Franklin D.

Roosevelt said of his own acres at Hyde Park, "but the land has just plain run out—and now I am putting it into trees in the hope that my great grandchildren will be able to try raising corn again." [13]

The dust bowl prompted the establishment of the Soil Conservation Service, and a nation-wide program (so far entailing over $15 billion in federal expenditures alone) to conserve soil resources has been in place ever since.

And yet erosion continues to be a crucial problem for U.S. agriculture. In 1977, just two years after the Council on Environmental Quality assured that "a new dustbowl is unlikely," there were a good many farmers in the West and Midwest who were hardpressed to tell the difference between the mid-thirties and the mid-seventies. Even though localized, wind erosion took its toll. In one Kansas town, streetlights had to be turned on at 10 a.m. when visibility approached zero from the dust. Paul Wilcoxen, a wheat farmer in Hamilton County, Kansas, lost 40 percent of his crop. The dust smothered plants or, if not, they were pulled out of the ground by the wind. According to the Washington Post, some 17 million acres were severely damaged by the drought and additional land further damaged from the ravages of wind.

But erosion is not just a problem that occurs under severe weather conditions. In fact, it seems to be an almost "built-in" feature of our current agricultural system which is able to mask the short-term effects of soil loss through fertilizer and other productivity enhancers. "At the moment," says Cornell University's David Pimentel, "we're taking out 1 inch of topsoil every eight to ten years on the average. The thing is, we could easily slow erosion to the rate at which new topsoil is being created from the bedrock, which is about 1 inch per century under agricultural conditions." [14] Although the techniques for reducing the rate of erosion are well known, the economic treadmill on which most farmers operate doesn't make it easy for them to adopt soil conserving practices.

Many farmers, forced to maximize production in the short-term have even given up some of the traditional, time-tested conservation practices that had been in common practice for decades. "Back in the 1930s, when the Soil Conservation Service first was established," writes M. Mitchell Waldrop, "most of the corn crop was planted in rotation with other crops. Now, only 40 to 45 percent is planted this way because continuous cropping is economically more efficient. Yet erosion jumps 25 to 30 percent with continuous cropping." [15]

The ever-increasing size of farm machinery has also prompted backsliding on conservation practices. Some farmers have reduced use of contour plowing simply because some of today's big tractors do not have the maneuverability needed to establish optimum contours. Similarly, shelterbelts have been removed on many farms in order to accommodate the big machines, and to make room for central-pivot irrigation equipment which operates on a radius—not the traditional rectangular field lines of the shelterbelt.

Nationwide, according to the 1977 National Resource Inventories, erosion removes 5.3 billion tons of soil from the country's privately owned agricultural land each year. It is estimated that, on the average, 4.7 tons of topsoil erode from each acre of cropland each year. When cropland planted in grasses (which provides greater erosion protection) is not considered, the average erosion rate is 5.8 tons per acre per year—which is above the 5 ton per acre rate which USDA considers to be the maximum soil loss tolerance rate (the rate of soil loss which can be sustained without threatening future produc-

tivity). Even with this modification the severity of erosion is still understated. The fact is, one-third of all cropland is eroding at more than 5 tons per acre per year, and
48 million acres—about 10 percent—lose 14 tons per
acre per year, or more.

Although it is difficult to quantify erosion's nationwide effects on productivity, USDA estimates that potential corn and soybean yields on some Midwestern
soils could be reduced by 15 to 30 percent by the year
2030. According to the National Association of Conservation Districts, present erosion rates may have an equivalent impact on production as removing 1.25 million acres
of cropland from production each year.[16]

Does it Matter?

Economists and resource specialists no doubt will continue to argue endlessly into the future about just how
much land prudence would suggest should be kept available for agriculture. Even now, a curious kind of re-
visionism is being heard in some quarters. "If things
really are as tight as NALS claims they are," one un-
named economist told the *Journal of Soil and Water Conservation*, "preserving farmland won't help much." [17]
But there is no longer reason to doubt that U.S. farmland
is not just a private resource, or even a national resource
of strategic significance—although it is these too. It truly
has become an international resource of transcedent importance.

Accordingly, the thorny question arises as to what
responsibility this generation has to protect a resource of
such value for the benefit of other countries and of future
generations here and abroad. In this regard, demand projections and forecasts of land needs may even confuse
the matter. For the policy maker trying to determine

what course of action should be taken—or even whether
action is needed—the range of forecasts that now exist is
so wide, and the assumptions behind them so various, as
to make most projections essentially meaningless, leav-
ing him with the same moral dilemma with which he
started.

An idea of the limitations of using demand models as
policy tools is suggested by a USDA demand projection
carried out for the so-called "Global 2000 Report." The
projection, based on trends through 1975, estimated that
the highest level of export demand for grain by the year
2000 was likely to be 157 million metric tons. The only
problem with this was that, by the time the report was
published in 1980 by the U.S. Department of State and
the Council on Environmental Quality, exports had already reached 164 million metric tons.[18]

Slightly closer to the mark may be an analytical concept that resource economists call "opportunity costs,"
which are the costs incurred by utilizing a resource today
in such a way that keeps the resource from being available for use in the future. Thus, a future cost can be
calculated for the three million acres of agricultural land
that are converted into housing, water reservoirs, highways and other development each year which are, for all
practical purposes, never going to be available for agriculture again. Nor can they produce feedstock for alcohol
fuels, or substitutes for strategic and essential materials
that are now imported if international sources of supply
become too costly or unreliable.

"You can probably convince yourself," says NALS
Executive Director Robert Gray, "that losing a million
acres of cropland out of a 540 million-acre base is indeed
a very small percentage in any given year, perhaps hard
to get excited about. But over four years, if you lose 4
million acres, if it happens to be land of moderate pro-

ductivity, that land would produce about the same amount of grain that is committed each year to foreign-assistance programs by all donor nations in the world. From the viewpoint of the world's needy people, setting aside 4 million acres in Iowa for use later in the century would indeed be viewed as significant."[19]

To view the matter in narrowly economic terms, therefore, is to risk missing the point: for economics can neither define, measure or assign responsibility in a matter that is ultimately a question of ethics. Inevitably, a country that has a land base capable of supplying 10 or 15 percent of the world's food supply must come to grips with the issue of whether it also has an obligation to protect and maintain that resource as best it can.

8

Productivity and the Ecology of Agriculture

"There are two ways of increasing food supply," Lester Brown, President of the Worldwatch Institute, has observed. "One is by increasing yields, and the other is by increasing the cropland area."[1] A key problem for those that are trying to understand how much agricultural land we may need in the coming decades is that yields are not behaving the way they did in the years following World War II. During the 1950s and 1960s, increases in yield per acre were steady and reasonably predictable. This, coupled with moderate export demands, consequently kept land needs predictable—and conservative.

But the 1970s—and especially the first half of the 1970s—saw a sharp change in the behavior of yields. In 1972 yields reached a high point that was not to be surpassed again until 1978. Then, in 1973 and 1974, they plummeted at the same time as world demand for U.S. food skyrocketed. After 1975, yields began to rebound, and bumper crops began to appear again—and did not slacken until bad weather in 1980 once again caused a decline in the rate of increase.

In recent years, the existence of bumper crops has had much more to do with the greatly increased amount of land in production than they have with increased yields per acre. The contrast between the 1970s and 1960s could not be more striking. "About three quarters of the overall growth in output in the 1970s was accounted for by bringing additional land into cultivation; crop yield increases from better and more intensive management accounted for about one quarter," notes the National Agricultural Lands Study. "The growth in the volume of production in the 1960s came entirely from gains in crop yields. In that decade, the acreage planted to crops actually declined .2 percent annually."[2]

The topsy turvy patterns of agricultural production in the last decade has dampened the optimism of those who think that the trend lines for yields can always be ever upward. Today, there is a kind of "hide-and-seek" game going on between yields and land, says Philip Raup. "What we are losing—what would be critical if we lost—would be the continued capacity to intensify."[3]

Are we in fact losing that capacity? Behind the statistics of agricultural production lie so many interacting economic, environmental and resource factors—climate, land, water supply and quality, energy, crop genetics, fertilizer and other inputs—that analysis is exceptionally difficult. A change in any one of these factors (either up or down or even no change when other factors do change) can have great effects on production in general. But there is good reason to suspect that the discontinuities—apparent ahistorical changes in the relative relationships among climate, land used for agriculture, and yields—which began to occur in the 1970s—are not over. "If the rate of productivity growth is indeed slowing," warns the USDA Study, *A Time to Choose*, "with the readily available land resource . . . largely committed, then the prospects for future expansion of production are not bright—absent a major breakthrough in production technology."[4]

Such breakthroughs are always a possibility. Right now, agronomists, using advances in genetic engineering made possible by primary research on recombinant DNA, are experimenting with new kinds of crops that could revolutionize agriculture to a degree that ultimately might exceed that of the Green Revolution of the 1950s and 1960s. Even so, according to NALS, "those analysts most optimistic about future crop yield gains anticipate at least a decade's delay before there are widespread on-farm benefits from research and development work now in progress."[5] Furthermore, given the unprecedented increase in world demand for our food, even major improvements in yields would not necessarily mean that farmers will once again begin to idle tens of millions of acres as they did in the 1950s and 1960s. Today, demand has become so intense that high yields can no longer be considered a substitute for land.

To get at the relationship between yields and land, it may be useful to think of agricultural production not in the classical mode of economics (Production = Land + Labor + Capital) but in a way that emphasizes the ecological relationships between the resource base and the environmental constraints that act upon it. Thus, with a slight redefinition of terms, it may be possible to come up with an alternative formula that may in some ways ring truer for today's conditions: Production is the result of interactions between climate (C), the land base (L) and the technical means (T)—including labor and capital— by which this environment (land and climate) is manipulated to produce food. Such a formula—P = CLT—has the virtue of providing an analytic framework for dealing with some of the more apparent discontinuities affecting agriculture today.

Climate

Some climatologists believe that the phenomenal increases in yields per acre that occurred during the 1950s
and 1960s owed as much to unusually favorable weather
conditions as to the more highly touted improvements in
agricultural technology. And these climatologists are
now concerned that we may be entering into a period of
more erratic (but, in an historic sense, perhaps more
"normal") weather patterns which could adversely affect
agricultural production. If so two major effects for the
land could be anticipated: if climatic trends outside the
U.S. are less favorable for agriculture, the importance of
the U.S. farmland as the world's granary will be even
further pronounced; if climate within the U.S. becomes
less favorable for agriculture, more land may be needed
to meet possible shortfalls.

For even the most casual observer, used to thinking
of food as something that comes from supermarkets, the
awesome power of the weather to affect agricultural production has been much in evidence of late. In one or
more years during the 1970s, the most important grain-
growing regions of the world—the U.S. Corn Belt, the
Great Plains of the U.S. and Canada, the Soviet Ukraine,
Australia and South Asia—were afflicted by unfavorable
weather that resulted in disasterous crop failures.

In 1974, the American Midwest suffered what Earl
Butz, then Secretary of Agriculture, called a "triple
whammy" of spring floods, summer drought, and early
fall frost. With world food reserves falling below the
danger point, and prices rising, the idea that modern
agriculture had somehow managed to protect itself from
the weather began to be questioned profoundly.

Again, in 1977, the weather was front page news.
The winter of 1976-1977 was characterized by severe

cold in the East (coldest, in point of fact, since the founding of the Republic), drought in the West and the Midwest, and mild temperatures as far north as Southern Alaska. But the summer was one of the two or three hottest in the last 100 years over much of the United States. That year, the drought resulted in the complete failure of the corn crop in some areas of Iowa.

Is there a trend in these occurrences, or are they merely random events, neither more nor less likely to be repeated in the next decade or so? That question is now receiving a great deal of attention from climatologists. To understand their concerns, it is useful to separate climatic occurrences into short-term trends (a matter of decades) and long-term trends (a matter of centuries or millennia). In the short-term, there can be dramatic changes in the weather from year to year which will not necessarily affect the long-term trend.

Most climatologists are hesitant about making long-term predictions about climatic change: equally plausible theories and scenarios exist which suggest that the earth will continue to cool as natural forces move it towards another Ice Age, or become warmer as a consequence of human activities that may affect climatic conditions. While the long-term trend is murky, most climatologists do believe that the earth *is* moving into a period of increased climatic variability—which for immediate practical purposes may be far more important than whether the eventual climate many decades or centuries from now will be warmer or cooler than it is today.

As climatologist R. H. Shaw puts it, "From the standpoint of agriculture, it is the short-term fluctuations around the climatic norm that is of greatest importance. Long term changes give some chance for technological change; short term 'climatic iterations' do not." [6]

The problem is that modern agriculture is not immune to fluctuations in climate even though in the recent past it has relied on climatic stability for sustaining high levels of food production. Many of the selected hybrid varieties of crops that have shown such pronounced increases in yields were developed to be suited for a climate that, from around 1955 to 1970, was highly favorable to agriculture, and less erratic than climatic conditions that prevailed between 1930 and 1955. These

favorable conditions included slightly reduced mean summer temperatures and increased rainfall.

Although these new crop varieties are suited for a wider range of conditions than traditional varieties, they are susceptible to extremes in weather patterns. Notes Shaw, "The combination of better crop varieties, fertilizers, etc., has produced a stronger, deeper-rooted plant that is better able to withstand stress conditions. . . . Under good weather conditions, production is much higher. Under conditions of mild to moderate stress, improved technology has helped to ameliorate stress conditions. Yet, in central Iowa in 1977 we lost a lot of our corn crop to severe drought. There simply was not any corn to pick. The only thing that would have saved that crop was irrigation."[7]

In fact, many midwestern and even eastern farmers are now installing "emergency irrigation" systems to give them the back-up to deal with just such situations. But if it is true that we have entered into a period of more variable weather, the farmer, not knowing whether the next year will bring bumper crops or no crop worthy of mention, will be motivated to plant the land as fully as possible. This, in turn, can have profound effects on the effective demand for land.

Limits of the Chemical Fix

If climate is a factor in production over which a farmer sometimes has very little control, this does not mean that the effects of environmental forces cannot be mitigated; they commonly are. Fertilizers, irrigation, mechanized planting, cultivating and harvesting, the use of pesticides and genetically improved strains, and conservation practices designed to optimize use of soil and water resources—all these technological maneuvers, and more, permit farmers to outfox the exogenous forces of nature (and human kind) by manipulating the agricultural environment.

Yet several worrisome aspects of agricultural technology stand out. Fertilizers, for example, can make up for reductions in the quantity of the land and the quality of the soil by increasing yields per acre. There are difficulties, however. For one thing, the application of chemical fertilizers can reach the point of diminishing returns. In the view of Lester Brown, of the Worldwatch

Institute, this point has arrived, or nearly so, for the United States. According to one research project, Brown writes, "At application rates of 40 pounds of nitrogen fertilizer per acre, each pound of nitrogen . . . increased the production of corn by about 27 pounds. As nitrogen applications approached 200 pounds, however, the weight of additional corn produced scarcely equaled the weight of the additional fertilizer added. Since the cost per pound of nitrogen fertilizer is several times that of corn, financial loss began to be incurred at application rates of between 120 and 160 pounds per acre." These application rates are not uncommon in the United States. In fact, Brown concludes, "farmers in the agriculturally advanced nations . . . are far up on the curve, with crop yields relatively unresponsive to additional chemical fertilizer."[8]

This finding does not mean, however, that fertilizer use can be drastically cut back with the expectation that yields will remain the same. It does mean that the use of *more* fertilizer to make up for land shortage or climate problems (or both) may have little effect.

Another difficulty in technological dependency on fertilizer use is the possibility that domestic supplies of phosphate may be limited. Since there is no substitute for this mineral in a fertilizer regimen, the importance of U.S. reserves is great. Though world reserves are twenty times as large as U.S. deposits, they are located in countries with whom advantageous trade agreements may be problematical. What is of concern in mining U.S. phosphate deposits is that they are located primarily in Florida (78 percent of U.S. production), where strip mining operations have caused serious environmental damage and may have to be modified.

Fear of shortage, plus increases in mining costs, together with increases in energy costs for making "super-phosphate" out of phosphate rock—an extremely energy-intensive process—have been among the factors accounting for the price of fertilizer going up so steadily in recent years. The result is that the use of fertilizers on American farms may be cut back. As the price of petroleum based fertilizer rises in relation to crop prices, the high price encourages farmers to cut back on fertilizer application, and hence they may expect some reduction in yield.

Irrigation

Another technological maneuver—irrigation agriculture, which produces some 27 percent of all crops on just 12 percent of the cropland base—accounts for some 80 percent of *all* water consumption in the West. In the years ahead irrigation agriculture faces some serious problems.

In several areas of the West, most notably west Texas, irrigation agriculture is taking much more water from aquifers than is being replenished naturally. In Gaines County, Texas, the water level in the Ogallala aquifer has dropped 12.8 feet in the last ten years. Groundwater depletion coupled with increasing costs of pumping water, has resulted in the abandonment of 100,000 acres of Pecos River Valley cropland in the last few years.[9] Another serious problem is build up of salts in irrigated land from repeated irrigation.

Western agriculture is also facing stiff competition from urbanization and energy development for the region's limited water supplies. The City of Tucson, for example, is trying to augment its water supplies by purchasing irrigated acreage, thus acquiring the water rights that go with it. So far, according to the U.S. Council on Environmental Quality, the city has purchased about

12,000 acres of farmland, and anticipates that it will need to purchase an additional 36,000 acres by 1985. This will essentially eliminate irrigation agriculture around the city.[10] Similarly, about 50,000 acres of irrigated land around Pueblo and Colorado Springs, Colorado, have been retired in order to meet urban water needs.

Some western communities recognize the need not only to stretch their water supplies as far as they can but also to make some accommodation with agriculture. An example is Northglenn, Colorado, a suburb of Denver. Rather than condemning irrigation water for municipal use as some other Colorado communities have done, Northglenn has entered into an agreement with local irrigators to recycle their water, and return it to them. The approach is intended to achieve several goals— keeping urban growth within sustainable levels, protecting nearby agriculture, and reducing water pollution.[11]

Even as western communities are becoming more sensitive to the water needs of agriculture, there is an added demand posed by new energy development. The U.S. Department of Energy has identified five western regions which may encounter water shortages in the future due to the added competition for this resource from energy and industrial development. Their report notes that "obtaining water supplies for new energy facilities in (these) water short regions could involve availability and institutional conflicts with other users."[12]

The problems with the water regime in the West are significant enough to be producing a major ecological event—desertification. An estimated 225 million acres in the West already are thought to have undergone severe desertification, which is characterized by lowered water tables, reduction of surface waters, salinization of water supplies, and severe erosion. Twice this acreage is currently threatened by desertification.[13] While there have been many grandiose plans to increase western water supplies through massive diversions of far away rivers, desalinization plants, or even transport of icebergs, these are not likely to occur within the foreseeable future, if at all. Thus, there is real uncertainty whether the West can sustain current levels of population growth, accommodate massive new energy development, and still maintain (let alone increase) its irrigated acreage in production.

Energy Costs

Farmers are as dependent on energy as everyone else. Fuel is needed for irrigation, and to power most other farm operations. Since 1910 the overall fuel energy requirement for food production has risen from roughly zero to a factor of nine—meaning that today it takes nine units of fuel energy to produce one unit of food energy.[14] "In effect," writes energy expert Wilson Clark, "agriculture today has shifted in a very real sense from soil to oil."[15]

In the view of Rene Dubos, "efficiency cannot be measured only in terms of agricultural yields. Another criterion is the amount of energy required for the production of a given amount of food. And when agriculture is judged on this basis, its efficiency is often found to be very low."[16]

Large amounts of fuel energy are used throughout the food system: from farm machinery (to manufacture it and to run it), to produce fertilizer and pesticides, to transport agricultural products, and to store, package, and market them. As energy costs have risen steeply, effects are felt throughout this manifold system. But none are so dramatic as those on the farm itself. Said one Pecos Valley, Texas, farmer bitterly, "In 1975, we were paying 31 cents per thousand cubic feet for natural gas. Today, those of us who are farming—and I'm not one—are paying $1.85 per thousand cubic feet. Virtually, nothing we can grow will pay out a profit at this expense." The valley needs gas to pump water up from the river. Without water, agriculture is no longer viable. Concluded the area's largest farmer, "The high cost of energy . . . has destroyed agriculture in this valley." [17]

The Pecos Valley example illustrates how the kind of inefficiency Rene Dubos describes can diminish even the agricultural land base itself in certain instances. Should such events continue, the effect may be felt in total agricultural output.

Energy costs—especially costs related to shipping—also may have some surprising implications for the geography of where food is grown. In the early decades of this century, the large cities of the East were surrounded by vegetable belts that met most of the in-season needs of local residents. With refrigeration, the rise of the trucking industry, and the large supermarket chains, California (which now produces 25 percent of the country's vegetables) was able to compete successfully for eastern markets.

But with the increase in transportation costs, western growers are now threatened. "It is transportation costs that have risen the most, and hurt the most," says agricultural economist Eric Thor. "People think that it just affects the cost of food, but the big effect is on market structure, where the food is grown, and where it is sold." [18] Two years ago, according to Thor, lettuce shipped from California to the East Coast was still roughly competitive with lettuce grown in New Jersey or Maryland. But shipping costs have doubled since then, making the competitive stance of Western growers more problematical.

Other Constraints

Additional inroads on productivity are projected because of another agricultural dependency—powerful herbicides, insecticides, and fungicides. Reduced yields come about to some degree for economic reasons, as pesticides become more expensive, requiring farmers to cut back on use, and for legal reasons—direct statutory restraints on their use. Theo F. Moriak estimates that "environmental restraints" alone can cut into expected growth of U.S. feed grain output per acre by 2.7 percent and wheat by 4.1 percent.[19]

This problem in turn relates to genetic weakness and vulnerability in many basic U.S. crops. Without heavy doses of pesticides (along with fertilizers, irrigation, and mechanized cultivation), monocultural planting of hybrid species far removed from their native germplasm sources can become highly susceptible to endemic predators—blight, rusts, insects.

Writes Garrison Wilkes of the University of Massachusetts, "Never before in human history have there been comparable monocultures (dense uniform stands) of billions of genetically similar plants covering thousands of acres." According to Wilkes, this practice leads to higher yields but only at a greater risk of crop failure, such as the wheat stem rust of 1954, which destroyed 25 percent of the bread wheat crop that year, and the 1970 corn blight which wiped out 20 percent of that crop.[20]

Although disease-resistant varieties can be developed, the hybridization required to produce high-yielding, disease-resistant varieties brings on its own problem, which Wilkes calls "genetic erosion." This arises when native seed stocks are lost and forgotten in the rush to create new hybrids. The native germplasm resources can only be stored in living systems. "The native varieties can become extinct once they are dropped in favor of introduced seed," says Wilkes. "Quite literally, the genetic heritage of a millenium in a particular valley can disappear in a single bowl of porridge."[21] Wilkes and others fearing "genetic wipeout" are now pleading for greater diversity of planting and for improved germplasm "banks" to store the genetic information that remains so that the genetic linkage with hardy native stocks can be maintained.

It is, of course, quite possible to find potential disasters lurking at every turn in an examination of modern agricultural technology. There are many who believe that the problem is that agricultural technology is not modern enough. The five troublespots discussed—fertilizers, irrigation, energy, pesticides, and genetics—do seem to show that present technologies may be reaching a point of diminishing returns, if not an outright backlash. This problematical future, added to a problematical future relating to climate and land indicates a prudent concern that under present technology, agricultural "efficiency" may be nearing the top of the curve in developed nations.

New Approaches to Farm Management

The productivity prognosis can change at any time, however, given new breakthroughs in technology and more sophisticated farm management. One example is the so called "conservation tillage"—involving either minimum tillage, or no tillage, which means plugging seeds into unbroken earth. The advantages of these conservation tillage systems were immediately apparent when they were first tested: fewer trips over the field meant that vast amounts of energy could be saved in comparison to land that had to be repeatedly cultivated;

less exposure of the soil meant that large areas of sloping land could be brought into production without fear of unacceptable levels of erosion; and in some cases "double cropping" became possible. But there were also disadvantages. Selective herbicides to control weeds in ways that would not have pernicious side effects, as well as acceptable and appropriate cultural methods of applying them, would be needed. Moreover, according to Neil Sampson of the National Association of Conservation Districts, crop varieties that performed well on a tilled field did not respond well to the cool, wetter environment that resulted when crop residues remained on the surface.[22] In addition, tillage equipment often broke down under the added strain of the residues.

But many of these problems were overcome—the herbicides being an exception—as equipment manufactures and seed producers responded to the obvious interest of farmers in conservation tillage by developing specialized seeds and equipment. Most recently, local soil and water conservation districts have been obtaining special equipment to loan to farmers to test conservation tillage techniques. As a result of this interaction, conservation tillage has exceeded expectations of even five years ago, and is, according to Sampson, the country's fastest growing soil conservation practice.

More efficient use of resources by farmers may not increase total agricultural production, but can help to cut costs and help reduce the impacts of industrial agriculture on the environment. According to *Chemical and Engineering News*, farmers are becoming much more adept at managing agricultural inputs (such as fertilizer, fuel, and pesticides) to keep costs within bounds. "When nitrogen was quite cheap," David Pimentel told the magazine, "growers would apply it in the winter, where there was a lot of surplus labor and equipment. Nobody cared that it was soluble and that lots of it was lost in the spring runoff. But now the price is up by a factor of four or five, so you apply it during the spring and summer when the crops can make most use of it."[23] Integrated pest management, which combines biological control of pests with judicious use of pesticides, is also catching on—albeit somewhat more slowly than some might expect.

One of the most startling indications of adjustment by farmers to the costs of energy and chemical intensive agriculture has been the recent emergence of organic farming as an important farm management alternative. Long considered a kind of fringe movement by the agricultural mainstream, the organic farm received a boost in July 1980 when USDA released a report which suggested that for many farmers organic farming has become a plausible economic alternative.[24]

On the Distant Horizon

Although not yet quite visible, unprecedented breakthroughs in agricultural technology are expected by many agronomists in the years to come. One of the most promising of these—made plausible by the tremendous advances in DNA research—is manipulation of DNA to produce plant varieties with characteristics that plant geneticists believe could survive, or even thrive, under seemingly adverse conditions. Writes Peter S. Carlson and Caroline G. Hoisington in the *Antioch Review:* "The Green Revolution technology was a 'package' deal in that fertilizers, insecticides and irrigation were generally required to allow the high-yielding varieties to out-yield (or sometimes even to meet the yields of) local varieties. Work is now being directed toward production of varieties without such requirements."[25] Breakthroughs in the photosynthetic efficiency of plants, and in the ability of plants to incorporate and utilize nitrogen are also seen as possible by some researchers.

And there are many other possibilities. For example, should it be found that cloud seeding is possible without drying out Farmer Peter to rain on Farmer Paul, weather modification techniques might develop as an important approach to environmental manipulation. Large-scale greenhouse agriculture may even become possible given new ways to reduce construction costs and energy use, thus obviating climate problems altogether.

A philosophically opposite school of agrarians, who espouse farming based on methods used by medieval French monks (the "French intensive method"), also argue that land can be made to give up greater yields than current agricultural practice permits. On experimental plots, researchers have found that by digging deep, using quantities of manure and mulch, planting close, and providing plenty of tender loving care, a diningroom-sized (10 by 12.5 ft.) plot can feed an individual for a year with enough left over for the goat.[26]

Meanwhile, a Japanese scientist, Hiroshi Johno, has undertaken experiments which suggest that neither vast amounts of land, water, or even tender loving care are really needed for growing crops in abundance. Using vinyl sheets, water-and-fertilizer tubes, and computer programming, Johno believes he has proven that "man can now fully turn the deserts and steppes, the barren and unproductive wastelands . . . into fertile farmlands teeming with lush vegetables and other plants . . . while all the existing farmlands will transform themselves into first rate agricultural areas, regardless of the degree of richness of their soils."[27]

If such exotic breakthroughs occur, it will take years for them to be used in a practical way by U.S. farmers. A more likely prospect is that for the foreseeable future no great technological change will revolutionize U.S. farming. Indeed, if there is a single theme that lies behind the current environmental and technological status of agriculture, it is that the land can no longer be viewed as a relatively unimportant factor in production as compared to technology. That the land is important might seem scarcely more than a truism. Yet, so remarkable were the technological advances in post-Depression agriculture that this was all but forgotten for a time. Now, the National Agricultural Lands Study has established that tens of millions more acres may have to be cropped even if yields increase as quickly as they did in the 1960s. The problem is to get people to believe it.

9

The Energy Overlay

The suspicion that agriculture in the United States has entered a new and more troubled era is only now receiving much currency, for it is not intuitively obvious that an industry that breaks foreign trade records eleven years in a row could be in trouble. For energy, the break between eras was sharp, and immediately recognized: the oil embargo of 1973, and the gas lines that called people's attention to it, triggered the most hurtful inflation experienced by the U.S. in modern times, and every one knew about it.

In a matter of months, petroleum price and supply instability emerged to become the pre-eminent domestic policy issue of the decade. And proposals for grand solutions to our energy problems have been coming thick and fast—first Project Independence, then the Energy Mobilization Act, then the Energy Mobilization Board and the Synfuels Corporation, and now, supply-side decontrol plus various measures to encourage new capital formation, along with relaxation of environmental and other regulations to inspire a massive energy hunt within our borders.

The trouble is, as ecologist Garrett Hardin's quotable phrase has it, "You can never do just one thing." The economic and political realities of energy may seem to dictate more oil wells, the development of oil shale, new conversion facilities, more coal stripping, more hydroelectric plants, and even pressing renewable resources into service—biomass in the form of row crops, trees and various waste products turned into energy. But, it is the land that is the "base" for this contemporary policy of energy-getting, and it is the land whose uses, appearance, and prior productivity could be dramatically affected if the plans now pinned to the drawing boards of corporate and governmental energy officials are put into effect.

Although this potential for disruption of agriculture has been almost completely ignored by energy planners, it has not gone unnoticed among the farmers themselves. In some areas of the country, farmers have resorted to threats of violence and even actual violence when new energy projects would affect their land adversely. Perhaps the most spectacular and disconcerting example of this concerns incidents of sabotage by farmers along a 430 mile powerline that transmits electricity from a power plant near Bismarck, North Dakota, to the Twin Cities of Minneapolis-St. Paul.

As described by Barry M. Casper and Paul David Wellstone in their fascinating case study of the conflict, *Powerline: The First Battle in America's Energy War,*[1] the controversy began as a peaceful protest in 1974 when a number of Minnesota farmers discovered that two power co-ops (ironically financed by low interest loans from the U.S. Department of Agriculture's Rural Electric Administration) were seeking approval for an extra-high voltage powerline which would cross a good many miles of productive farmland. As successive legal challenges to the project failed, antagonism of farmers mounted—so much so that, by 1978, when the last legal challenges to the project fell through, the Governor had to call in 200 state troopers to prevent angry farmers from interfering with contruction of the line.

The conflict produced a good deal of national media attention during its construction, but less so since its completion when, according to the *Powerline* authors, "an unexpected and unprecedented phase of guerrilla warfare" began. By September, 1980, 14 of the giant transmission line towers had crashed to the ground, as a result of "bolt weevils" who simply unpinned the towers from their moorings. In addition, hundreds of insulators along the line—damaged by gun-fire—have had to be replaced.

While the sabotage to the line is indefensible, a siting process more sensitive to the problems of farmers would no doubt have reduced the potential for conflict. Almost certainly, if the project were proposed today, a route less destructive of farmland would be chosen: in 1977, the Minnesota legislature amended the siting law to include impacts on farmland in siting criteria, and, in 1978, the U.S. Secretary of Agriculture instructed all USDA agencies (including the REA) to avoid funding projects which would indiscriminately and needlessly destroy high quality agricultural land.

Transmission line siting conflicts between utilities and farmers have also arisen in New York State, Illinois, Iowa, and other places. In South Dakota, agricultural opposition to a proposed coal slurry pipeline was so intense that the state's Attorney General in 1975 predicted a need for federal marshalls along every mile of its length if the project were to proceed. Other kinds of energy projects—hydroelectric facilities, surface mines and power plants—have drawn vehement opposition from farm groups when these projects would adversely affect agricultural land.

The unprecedented quantity of new energy projects now proposed suggests that these confrontations presage what is to come. Surveys by the U.S. Department of Interior's Bureau of Mines,[2] undertaken in 1976 and 1977, identified 1,333 major new major energy projects at the planning or proposal stage—including 400 coal mines, 450 electric generating plants, 115 uranium mines, 53 oil refineries, 43 coal conversion facilities, and 46 geothermal facilities. Not all of these projects will be completed, or even reach the construction phase. But in some cases those that are undertaken could have significant effects on local and regional agriculture.

It is very difficult to estimate just how much land in the aggregate might be needed for fossil fuel development and other kinds of energy facilities in the future. Despite the fact that the energy industry already occupies more land than any other heavy-industrial activity, energy planners have paid virtually no attention to the potential land impacts of their "energy future" scenarios.

Proposed federal energy plans, such as President Nixon's Project Independence, President Ford's Energy Independence, and President Carter's National Energy Plan, have generally devoted only a few paragraphs to the land impacts of energy development, and none of the scenarios have specifically addressed the potential effects of energy development on agricultural land availability. Yet, under the three scenarios a significant amount of rural land would be affected—ranging from about 270,000 acres per year under Carter's National Energy Plan, to over a million acres a year under the original Project Independence Report.[3] Even more land would be diverted to surface mining, waste disposal sites, and other energy-related land uses considered to be temporary in nature.

Getting at the Coal

In the conflict between energy and agriculture, the one area where federal policy makers seem to have come down on the side of agriculture—albeit tentatively—is surface mining. Over ten million acres in the United States are underlain by potentially strippable coal reserves, according to the U.S. Department of Interior's Office of Surface Mining Reclamation and Enforcement.[4] About a quarter of these reserves are located under prime agricultural land in the Midwest and other states east of the Mississippi River. Additional reserves are located under western alluvial valley floors, which tend to have soils, topography and water availability favorable for agriculture.

Most energy development scenarios envision a major increase in surface mining in the coming years; thus, concern about adverse impacts on agriculture led to provisions in the Federal Surface Mining Control and Reclamation Act, enacted in 1977, calling for stringent reclamation requirements for prime agricultural lands and the alluvial valley floors. Difficulties in implementing this act, however, as well as legislative proposals to limit its scope, make its promise for protecting agricultural land resources uncertain at this time.

Relatively little land has yet been surface mined for coal. Over the long run, however, a substantial acreage could be required for surface mining. One study of energy development in eight Rocky Mountain states estimated that between 1000 and 1500 square miles could be disturbed by surface mining in these states alone by the year 2000, and up to 18 percent of the land area in some individual counties was seen as being subject to disruption.[5] Estimates of land needs for energy development over the next 50 years in the northern Great Plains—an area that includes Montana, North Dakota, South Dakota, Nebraska and Wyoming—range from a low of 240,200 acres to a high of 1,473,140 acres in 2035.[6]

In the Midwest, according to a report by the USDA's Economics, Statistics and Cooperatives Service,[7] about 226,000 acres of agricultural land are likely to be out of production because of surface mining in any given year between now and the year 2000, with lost agricultural income from these acres amounting to about $17 million per year.

The pace of Midwestern surface mining might increase more rapidly if the economics of the coal industry change, or if provisions in the federal surface mining legislation (and related state statutes) are modified to lessen reclamation requirements for prime farmland. Researchers at Iowa State University have developed an economical method for removing the high quantities of sulfur that characterizes the state's coal resources.[8] This sulfur, left in the coal, produces unacceptable levels of air pollution but when cleaned through the new process, can be burned in power plants without as much risk of breaking air pollution standards. With one third of Iowa underlain by coal seams, the potential for a revival of the coal industry may be great, given this technology, but so too is the potential for conflict with agriculture. Surface mining often is characterized as only a temporary disruption of the land, because of the potential for reclaiming the land for productive use after mining is completed. However, there has been an on-going argument about the overall success of reclamation practices, and uncertainty as to whether surface mined prime agricultural land can ever be returned to a fully productive state.[9]

Synthetic Fuels

Production of oil and gas substitutes (or synthetic fuels) from coal and oil shale is a frequently proposed means of reducing our dependency on foreign oil. The synthetic fuels industry is not yet well developed in this country, but interest in accelerating synfuels production is growing. In 1980, Congress created the Federal Synthetic Fuels Corporation to channel federal assistance to the synthetic fuels industry.

The impact of a major synthetic fuels program for agriculture has not been intensively studied. A July 1979 Department of Energy environmental analysis of siting issues for synthetic fuels identified 159 counties in 15 states with adequate coal reserves to support a 100,000 barrel per day synthetic fuel facility for 25 years. After factoring in air quality constraints, DOE narrowed this list to 41 counties in eight states—including 10 in Montana, 8 in Illinois, 7 in North Dakota, 6 in Wyoming, and 5 in West Virginia—which would appear to provide a "siting opportunity" for synfuels facilities. However, among the factors explicitly excluded from the analysis were: (1) "need for land use that is prohibited or that requires extensive reclamation, such as prime agricultural lands"; (2) "institutional transfer problem for water availability"; and (3) "cumulative impacts of large scale facilities and associated mining."[10] All of these omitted factors are, of course, centrally important for assessing the impact of a synfuels program on agriculture.

The Fight for Water

The U.S. Water Resources Council projects that water use for energy purposes could quadruple by the year 2000—from 3.8 billion gallons per day in 1975 to 16 billion gallons per day in the year 2000. There is thus a very real concern that the price of water can be "bid up" due to the twin competition from Sun-belt cities and new western energy facilities.

At present, irrigation accounts for 80 percent of all withdrawals from western water sources. Because agriculture has such a high stake in water resources, the purchase of water rights by energy companies has become a major regional issue. A National Academy of Sciences study flatly stated that "not enough water exists for large-scale conversion of coal to other energy forms— e.g., gasification or steam-electric power." [11] Many other studies undertaken in the 1970s suggested serious difficulties in accommodating the water needs of energy development without taking water away from irrigation agriculture. There have been dissenting opinions, of course, notably a 1980 U.S. General Accounting Office report which concluded that adequate water is available in the West for energy development "through at least the year 2000." While the caveat is disconcerting, since 2000 is now close at hand, GAO concluded that growth in western energy projects has not been as rapid as was previously expected, and that various energy technologies have not required as much water as was believed previously. A curious aspect of the report is that it did not discuss in any detail other water uses that compete with energy development—most especially irrigation. Aside from noting that provision of federal water would be an apparently more preferable option than procurement of agricultural water rights (an option the report describes as "politically sensitive and socially disruptive"), the report focuses almost exclusively on the physical availability of surplus federal water which could be diverted to energy use.

Most likely, the bidding away of water resources required by energy development has not yet reached, or even approached, its peak. When it does, increased prices or outright scarcity could make a significant dent in agricultural production capacity that is becoming increasingly dependent on dams and pipelines rather than rain. According to USDA, the annual increase in irrigated land is 700,000 acres per year. Ninety percent of this land is in the 17 western states where major new energy resources are located.

Air Pollution and Crop Yields

The potential for air pollution to affect crop yields has only recently received much attention, and generalization is difficult. But evidence is accruing that some crops in some areas are greatly affected. Studies undertaken by southern California researchers[12] under controlled conditions that allowed comparisons of crops exposed to ambient (polluted) air versus crops exposed to filtered (clean) air found sizeable reduction in yield in those crops exposed to the ambient air. Alfalfa yields declined 38 percent; blackeyed peas, 32 percent; lettuce, 42 percent; sweet corn, 72 percent; and radish, 38 percent. In Massachusetts, similar experiments showed yield reductions from ambient air pollution of 15 percent for alfalfa and sweet corn, 25 percent for beans, and 33 percent for tomatoes.

The effects of an increase in sulfur oxide levels that would accompany greater utilization of coal as an energy source is prompting considerable concern—especially given the drive to relax clean air standards to encourage the use of this fuel. A recent report published by the Department of Energy estimates that sulfur dioxide emissions from coal-fired utility boilers could increase by 15 percent by 1990 even if the federal Clean Air Act requirement were properly implemented. The effects of conversion to coal by other industries could be much greater—and increase up to 149 percent by 1990 over 1975 industrial emission. If less stringent emission requirements are permitted, as is now proposed, greater emissions can be expected.

Unfortunately, the effects of air pollution are not localized. Long range transport of air pollution, with subsequent deposition in distant areas—frequently 1000 kilometers away—has long been recognized to be a major air pollution problem in Scandinavia, where a significant amount of air pollution from industrial centers in Europe falls out as highly acidic rainfall. This acid rain is reported to have adversely affected aquatic life and forest growth, and has corroded building structures.

An increase in the acidity of rainfall has also been noted in several areas of the United States. Initially detected in the Northeast, the phenomenon has apparently spread westward and southward, so that it now extends from Illinois to the East coast. Increased acidity through dry deposition may also occur in the western United States as a consequence of the expected construction of a large number of coal-fired power plants in the coming years.

Nationwide estimates of the economic costs of air pollution in terms of vegetation damage and damage to buildings range from several hundred million dollars to $1.7 billion per year. Such estimates are based on acute air pollution episodes. In this regard, a recent report by the U.S. Environmental Protection Agency notes that "dollar losses incurred from long term, chronic, low level exposure of crops, forests, and natural ecosystems to air pollutants remain virtually unmeasured nationwide." [13] If crop yields are measurably affected by such chronic, low level exposure, however, the amount of land required to achieve a given level of agricultural production may need to be increased in the future. If the effect were, say, at 1 percent of yield, annually, as some suggest, this would have a rough equivalency to the annual loss of production from 3.5 million acres of cropland.

The Boomtown

The most celebrated effect of large-scale energy development—especially, in the interior western states—is the energy boomtown. One well-publicized example is Sweetwater County, Wyoming, which between 1970 and 1974 experienced a 19 percent annual population growth rate. The annual rate has now abated to a mere seven percent—a figure that in other places takes ten years to happen, not one. In 1970, Sweetwater County had one doctor per 1,000 population. By 1973, it had one doctor per 3,800. Suicide, alcoholism, child abuse, and divorce increased at alarming rates. Meanwhile housing, police and other public services, and commercial facilities were strained beyond capacity.

Despite the best efforts of policy makers and planners in these areas, the boomtown syndrome is likely to continue and to increase—especially in Colorado, California, Texas, Utah, and Wyoming—according to the Department of Interior and the Department of Housing and Urban Development. Colorado alone has 141 planned or proposed energy projects, according to Interior, that could create boomtown conditions.

According to the General Accounting Office, boomtown governments often have an almost total lack of expertise available to cope with growth. According to GAO, a survey of 131 communities likely to be affected by energy development revealed that few had any full-time planners, city engineers or town managers. Moreover, only a third of these communities have adopted any kind of comprehensive plan.

How is agriculture affected by boomtown growth? The question has not received much attention from planners, but the same kind of impermanence that pervades farming conducted on the urban fringe will also affect agricultural operations around energy boomtowns. Most new energy projects take place in rural areas, and the growth that results occurs in small towns and cities that previously were dominated by the needs of the agricultural industry. The favorable conditions for agriculture that preceded the boomtown may begin to give way: farm laborers may be attracted by higher paying jobs associated with the energy industry, local lending institutions may shift capital away from farming, traffic congestion may make farm business in town more time consuming, and the general ambiance of rural and small town life may break down.

The Need to Take Agriculture into Account

From the foregoing analysis, it seems clear that the unprecedented scope of energy development now being proposed in this country has the potential to do much mischief to agriculture. The direct mischief—the diversion of agricultural land to energy development—is easy to observe, but not necessarily the more important. The subtler, indirect effects—the bidding up of the price of irrigation water, possible declines in crop yields from air pollution, and the creation of a more unfavorable environment for agricultural activities—are not easy to quantify, but may, in the end, be more damaging.

Moreover, in the web of interconnections and ramifications that spread out from Hardin's admonition that you can never do just one thing, that potential damage to agriculture may come back to haunt energy policy as well. Who can say with assurance, for example, that the country's energy future will be better served by turning farmland in Illinois into surface mines that will produce coal that will in turn be converted into synthetic fuels? True, if federal reclamation requirements remain in effect, that land in twenty or thirty years might be returned to agricultural use once the coal is gone. But left in agricultural use all along, that farm could produce crops for exports that can help reduce trade deficits incurred from importation of foreign oil. Moreover, it might very well produce alcohol fuels that could help to reduce the oil imports themselves. And, with proper management, it could do this indefinitely.

10

Land and the Gasohol Question

Energy planners and policy makers have largely ignored the repercussions of their projects for agriculture—except in such instances when specific projects run up against political opposition from agricultural organizations. Such ignorance should not be casually dismissed as yet another example of bureaucratic befuddlement, for agricultural policy and energy policy now interact in complex and comprehensive ways. For nearly a decade U.S. agricultural exports—last year $40.5 billion—have played a crucial role in off-setting trade deficits incurred largely from oil imports. In effect agriculture helped pay for our energy. Now, the association may be more direct. In the future, biomass energy produced from agricultural and forest products very likely may make an important contribution to the country's energy budget.

Organic wastes and residues, crops, and wood can be burned directly as a fuel, or can be converted into other products, such as alcohol, which can be easily substituted for fossil fuels. With proper land management biomass feedstocks can be produced on a renewable basis; moreover, they are generally thought to produce less of a pollution hazard than fossil fuels which tend to have higher concentrations of sulfur.

Estimates of the potential contribution of biomass to the nation's energy needs vary significantly. Some believe that biomass energy use could be tripled by the year 2000, and that over the longer term, an even greater contribution to total energy needs can be realized.[1]

Wood by far provides the most significant amount of biomass-derived energy at present. Once the dominant source of fuel in this country, wood, by 1970, had declined to less than one percent of energy use. But it recently has undergone an unprecedented revival, as forest-product firms, homeowners, and even electric utilities strive to find cheaper alternatives to oil. Now, according to Nigel Smith of the Worldwatch Institute, wood's contribution to the country's energy budget has surpassed that of nuclear energy. He believes that wood energy use will increase by a factor of five by the end of the century.[2]

But it is another biomass energy source—ethanol, or grain alcohol—that is likely to have the most direct implications for agriculture, at least in the short run.

The Re-emergence of an Industry

Running cars, tractors and other machinery on alcohol—either to supplement gasoline, or as a substitute for it—is nothing new. Henry Ford built the Model T to run on either gasoline or alcohol, or any combination in between. During the Second World War, grain produced in Nebraska, Kansas and Illinois was converted into ethanol which was mixed with gasoline, and marketed at local gas stations as Argol. With U.S. oil supplies threatened, research on ethanol, as well as other petroleum substitutes, was also undertaken. For most of the automotive era, however, gasoline was so cheap and so readily available that the only publicly visible manifestation of alcohol fuels seemed to be the annual running of the Indianapolis 500, at which most of the cars have been fueled by methanol, or wood alcohol.

All that, of course, has now changed. First the farm states, then several other states began to provide incentives (such as reduced state sales taxes on gasoline) for gasohol—usually a blend of nine parts gasoline to one part alcohol. Then, in 1978, Congress followed suit by exempting gasohol from the $.04 per gallon federal sales tax on gasoline—equivalent to a 40 cent subsidy on every gallon of ethanol. The effect of the federal subsidy, together with major new initiatives announced by the Carter Administration in January 1980 to make loan guarantees available for fuel alcohol distilleries, was initially dramatic: from virtually no alcohol fuel production prior to 1978, ethanol production by the end of 1980 had climbed to nearly 150 million gallons per year—enough (when blended with gasoline) to produce 1.5 billion gallons of gasohol which is now marketed at over 3,000 gas stations throughout the country.

And a far higher level of production may be possible soon as new distilleries, able to be built in two or three years, come on line. By the end of 1980, the Farmers Home Administration had issued loan guarantees for 15 major new distilleries, capable of producing 246 million gallons per year. Under another federal program, the Department of Energy had tentatively approved loan guarantees for another nine plants, with a collective capacity of 215 million gallons. The loan guarantee program for new distilleries is one of the items that the Reagan Administration would like to delete from the federal budget, but exemption of gasohol at the pump from the federal gasoline tax will continue.

The long and short of it is that what was little more than a pipe dream on the part of midwestern and Great

Plains farmers just five years ago now has the potential to become a major industry. Ten years ago few analysts had the prescience or just plain luck to anticipate the phenomenal increase in world demand for U.S. food that would follow; fewer still seriously entertained the notion that, by the early 1980s, Americans in nearly every state would be able, if they choose, to fill their car's tank with fuel partially grown in Iowa. Yet the future course of the gasohol industry—whether it will boom or bust—is not much easier to predict today.

First of all, as this is written gasohol is in a momentary decline, which some believe suggests that the promise of the industry is lagging. But with a new round of OPEC price rises it could be that gasohol consumption may resume its upward climb.

Even so there are limits to how much alcohol fuel can be produced. With U.S. cars now consuming around 100 billion gallons of gasoline per year, even the most avid supporters of gasohol think it unlikely that the U.S. ever would be able to offset, say, 20 percent of its gasoline consumption through substitution of ethanol, as Brazil in fact is now doing. Moreover, as a creature of subsidy, gasohol still cannot compete on its own at the pump with gasoline. If the Reagan Administration succeeds in cancelling the loan guarantee programs for new distilleries, investors may be reluctant to assume the risk themselves—especially given the oil "glut" of 1981, which has temporarily dampened enthusiasm for gasohol.

There remain technical questions as well, about whether conversion of biomass into alcohol produces more energy than the conversion process itself consumes. Here also the prognosis is mixed. When standard agricultural practices and conventional distilleries are used, the net energy balance for ethanol is likely to be negative. But with adoption of energy-conserving farm practices, and more energy-efficient conversion processes, positive energy gains may be feasible. In any event, gasohol proponents think the net energy balance question misses the point, since gasohol can reduce imported petroleum use not only in automotive fuels but because other fuels—coal, wood, or crop residues—can be used to fire the distilleries. Thus, they see "gasohol" as a strategically important sagefuard against future oil embargos and OPEC price rises.

Will There be Enough Land?

Curiously enough, given the fact that a biomass fuel industry will depend upon the land, very little research has been conducted on how alcohol fuels production will affect the agricultural land base, and existing farm and forest uses. When the first "grand scenarios" for biomass energy began to appear in the mid years of the 1970s, it was still widely assumed that a very large quantity of highly productive land was either not being utilized or was underutilized for food and fiber production. Energy analysts, not yet privy to the radical escalation in land needs for agriculture that began in the early 1970s, spoke with confidence of the possibility of establishing a very large biomass energy industry through utilization of land then idled under government set-aside programs, or if that wasn't enough, by bringing into production some of the 266 million acres of land then thought to constitute our cropland reserves. Almost as soon as these early biomass "scoping" studies appeared, the much more pessimistic findings by the SCS about our limited cropland capabilities began to emerge. But energy planners, undaunted, continue cheerfully to assume that there is somehow a great deal of readily available and unused cropland out there on which biomass energy could be produced without affecting other kinds of agricultural production.

The reality is quite different. Grain for ethanol production is not being grown on newly established plantations put on vacant land, but is being produced from existing cropland. In fact, so far, the nascent alcohol fuel industry has been fed exclusively on a diet of agricultural commodities, such as corn and grain sorghum, that might otherwise have been destined to enter the world markets were it not for the partial embargo on grain (since suspended) to the Soviet Union that the Carter Administration announced at the same time it stepped up its commitment to alcohol fuels.

Although only a small amount of agricultural product is now used to produce ethanol—not yet enough in the opinion of USDA to have much influence on the price of food—there is good reason for concern about what might happen to food prices if the ethanol industry grows rapidly and continues to increase its use of agricultural commodities for feedstock. Cautions Lester Brown, in his report *Food or Fuel: New Competition for the World's Cropland:* "Within the food exporting countries, the short run attractions of converting exportable food surpluses into alcohol fuels are undeniable. Whether the longer term political effects will be as attractive is less clear. In a world that no longer has any excess food production capacity, the decision to channel foodstuffs into the production of automotive fuel will inevitably drive food prices upward. For the world's affluent, such rises in food prices may lead to belt tightening; but for the several hundred million who are already spending most of their meager income on food, continually rising food prices will further narrow the thin margin of survival." [3]

A Bridge to the Future?

USDA apparently views reliance on agricultural commodities for feedstock as a short term measure, since, in
the future it may be economically feasible to produce
alcohol (either ethanol or methanol) from wood, wood
wastes, and agricultural residues. In describing the
Carter Administration's alcohol fuels program to Congress in 1980, then Deputy Assistant Secretary of Agriculture Jim Williams explained this strategy as follows:
"The present availability of grains and other starch and
sugar crops which are readily fermentable represents
significant sources of biomass feedstocks for alcohol production. This should serve as a bridge until new technology will permit economic production of alcohol fuels
from cellulosic biomass such as crop and woody products, either as residues or grown specifically for energy
production."[4]

Williams reported progress with this technology, but
could not project when it would be available for commercial use in this country. But if the bridge is crossed soon,
a potentially enormous reservoir of wood, wood wastes
and agricultural residues may be tappable for feedstock.
That, at least, was a conclusion of the U.S. Department of
Energy's Alcohol Fuels Policy Review, completed in
late 1979.[5]

Even with today's conversion technology, according
to the policy review, a theoretical maximum of 12.2 billion gallons of ethanol could be produced annually by
the year 2000 from food processing wastes, grains and
sweet sorghum (a high-sugar crop not currently produced in large quantities). If the more efficient conversion technology were to become commercially available,
however, a theoretical maximum of 42 billion gallons of
ethanol could be produced annually which by the year

2000 could reach 54 billion gallons. The theoretical potential for methanol would be even higher.

These are theoretical maximums, of course, and DOE does not anticipate such a major increase in alcohol fuel production. But production levels even a fraction of theoretically possible size could exert major pressures on the agricultural land base. In fact, DOE held that a realistic assessment of ethanol production through the mid-1980s would be 660 million gallons a year—which it thought would be achieved not by using marketable agricultural commodities (as so far has turned out to be the case), but by using food processing wastes, and distressed or substandard grain. Over the longer run, according to DOE, an "upper limit of 4.7 billion gallons of ethanol could be produced by bringing into production all existing grain land and by supplementing food processing wastes with sugar surpluses and fermentable municipal solid wastes." DOE cautioned—perhaps unnecessarily—that "achieving this limit would be expensive and would reduce the flexibility of U.S. agricultural land and restrict options for food production."[6]

Is There a Free Lunch?

One of the most intriguing aspects of the biomass energy issue is that the process of producing ethanol from grain can yield a high-protein content livestock feed called "distillers grain." Because both feed and fuel can be produced from the same crop, ethanol production and livestock feed production complement each other to some extent—a fact that became evident to the National Agricultural Lands Study when it tried to estimate cropland needs for ethanol production.

Looking over the various projections of future ethanol production, the NALS decided that it was reasonable to assume that between four and six billion gallons per year would be produced by 1990 as long as the real price of energy rises faster than the price of agricultural feedstocks. Such a level of production, according to NALS, would require between 15 and 23 million acres planted in corn. But as ethanol production expands, the ready availability of inexpensive distillers grain as a byproduct of this production would encourage a shift in land now used to produce soybean feed supplements into corn production. Thus, the net increase in land used to produce row crops for ethanol production would probably range between 7 and 11 million acres.[7]

Opinions differ about just how much distillers grain the livestock industry could absorb. Distillers grain is not a complete livestock feed; it reportedly results in less rapid weight gain than soybean meal, and is therefore not the preferred feed. Moreover, uncertainty exists about the effect of sudden increases in distillers grain on the price structure of feed supplements. Even so, proponents of gasohol production believe that it may be possible to utilize land now used for feedgrain production (about 105 million acres) for production of ethanol feedstock without greatly affecting current levels of livestock production.

Ecologist Barry Commoner and associated investigators at Washington University have reported an approach that they believe could meet current livestock production needs and still produce about eight quads of energy a year (roughly ten percent of *all* U.S. energy consumption). About 15 percent more land than is now used for feed grain production would be required. Most of this land would be used to produce crops (such as corn and sugar beets) that can be converted easily into ethanol. The distillers grain byproducts would then be fed to livestock, together with some hay. Manure from the livestock would, in turn, be used to produce methane gas. Remaining byproducts would be returned to the land as fertilizer.[8]

Another intriguing possibility is that special "energy" crops—plants that are especially useful for energy purposes—will be grown more extensively in the future. Sweet sorghum is not planted widely in the United States at present, but is considered by Department of Energy analysts to be a very promising potential source of ethanol feedstock because of its high sugar content. They estimate that 14 million acres of cropland planted with sweet sorghum would produce 8.3 billion gallons of ethanol a year. Genetic experimentation and plant breeding could also result in new varieties of plants with characteristics favorable for energy use. Moreover, an effort is now underway to identify plants that have an unusually high level of hydrocarbons that could be potentially tapped directly as a source of liquid fuel. One promising candidate species, *Euphorbia lathyris*, is naturally adapted to semi-arid conditions, and reportedly could produce the equivalent of 6.5 barrels of oil per acre on a renewable basis. If its promise were to bear out, land in the semi-arid Southwest might be used for sustained production of the plant.

The Decentralized Alternative

Regardless of how serious the nation's energy problems may be, or how technically sophisticated the "growing of energy" becomes, the potential impact of a major alcohol fuels industry on the quality and quantity of the agricultural land base needs more careful assessment than it has received thus far.

There is, however, an alternative to large scale industrial ethanol production, an alternative described by

James Clark, a Howard County, Maryland farmer and state senator.

"We all have to be as self sufficient as possible these days," Clark told the *Washington Post*. "I figure with two stills I can make four or five gallons of alcohol a day, which should be plenty for my needs." Clark is not talking about the kind of alcohol you drink—the alcohol he produces will be denatured by the time it is used, and besides, being a moonshiner is not quite consistent with his part time job representing his county in the state senate. Rather, he plans to use the alcohol to help fuel his tractors. Clark is not sure whether he'll save money producing his fuel on the farm: it takes a bushel of corn (at $3.00 per bushel) to produce two gallons of alcohol, and that doesn't cover the cost of the stills or the labor. "But one thing's certain," he adds: "I'll always have an available supply."[9]

Clark is in the vanguard of farmers trying to "grow" their own energy for on-farm use. According to the U.S. Treasury's Bureau of Alcohol, Tobacco and Firearms, the agency responsible for issuing permits for distilleries, only 18 small scale fuel alcohol distillery permits had been issued by the end of 1978. By October 1979, 700 permits had been issued. And, by March 31, 1981, 9,500 permits were in effect.

Many think that small-scale, decentralized technologies aimed at producing liquid fuels for on-farm use might pose less of a potential for confict with traditional markets for food, feed and fiber products than would industrial-scale operations. Still, a number of uncertainties exist about the practicality of on-farm fuel production. A recent "Gasohol" report by the Congressional Office of Technology Assessment (OTA) confirmed Clark's skepticism about the economics of on farm production, noting that "as an economically profitable venture . . . on farm ethanol production is, at best, marginal under present conditions." OTA stressed, however, that "for some farmers the cost and/or labor required to produce dry or wet ethanol may be of secondary importance. The value of some degree of energy self-sufficiency and the ability to divert limited quantities of corn or other grains when the price is low may well out-weigh the inconvenience and the cost." [10] Moreover, on-farm fuel production could become more practical in the future as relatively automatic and inexpensive distilleries become available.

Land Degradation

Although often characterized as an environmentally preferable alternative to fossil fuel use, large scale agricultural production of alcohol feedstocks (and even small scale production, for that matter) could result in serious erosion and soil fertility problems unless special care is taken.

If crop residues become an important source for ethanol production as technology for converting cellulosic materials into alcohol improves, a major potential for land degradation could arise. Crop residues are normally returned to the soil, where they play an important role in maintaining soil quality and preventing erosion. The extent to which they can be removed without unacceptably impairing the soil varies from place to place. But careful management practices will be needed to assure adequate consideration of soil conservation objectives.

A second land quality problem could arise if the demand for biomass feedstocks results in the utilization of poorer quality land for production of wood or agricultural crops. "Diversion of extensively managed pasture, range and forest to biomass production would less severely affect U.S. production than would the diversion of cropland or intensively managed pasture and forest land," writes Kathryn A. Zeimetz of the Department of Agriculture. "However, the extensively managed forage or woodlands generally have severe quality limitations which would also limit these lands' usefulness for biomass production. Lower biomass yields mean increased per unit costs of energy production. Subjecting marginal land to the high input levels and the repeated radical clearings necessary for acceptable biomass yields would greatly increase the danger of environmental degradation from non-point sources of pollution and erosion. Conservation practices would be costly." [11]

Will the Nature of Farming be Changed?

The alcohol fuels industry has arisen so suddenly that its full ramifications for agriculture can hardly be imagined. At this juncture, it is perhaps neither more nor less plausible to view the venture as a flash-in-the pan that will die down and fade if subsidies are cut and if gasoline prices hold fairly steady, or as a clear indication that in a decade the American agricultural system will include fuel as well as the traditional food, feed and fiber.

If the latter turns out to be the case, biomass energy production could be both a promising opportunity and a source of thorny problems for American agriculture. On the one hand, demand for feedstock could strengthen the market for agricultural products and enhance the profitability of farming, which in turn could also enhance agriculture's ability to compete successfully with non-agricultural uses for the same land base.

On the other hand, the increased demand for biomass feedstocks could bring out destructive competition between fuel and the traditional demands for food, feed and fiber. This could become a policy issue of the utmost importance in a world highly dependent on U.S. food exports. Moreover, significant land degradation problems could occur if the demand for feedstock results in over use of crop residues, or if large amounts of marginal land are introduced into production.

Furthermore, it is possible—even likely—that important structural changes in U.S. agriculture may occur if the needs of a large alcohol fuels industry are to be accommodated. It is one thing if alcohol fuels are produced by farmers for on-farm use, or if groups of farmers form cooperatives to distill ethanol for local or regional markets. It may be quite another if large commercial distilleries are built by energy conglomerates or other large corporations. In fact, many of the largest companies in the country (Mobil Oil, Westinghouse, Weyerhaeuser, ITT, Occidental Petroleum, and Conoco, among them) are seeking federal loan guarantees for alternative energy projects. Not all of these involve alcohol fuels, but the potential for a different kind of corporate presence in American agriculture is now beginning to appear.

Thus, it is well to keep in mind a cautionary note presented by former Secretary of Agriculture Bob Bergland to the Congress in 1979. Bergland warned against proceeding with a large scale commercial effort to produce ethanol without fully taking into account its potential to effect agriculture. The construction of distilleries to meet even a significant fraction of the ten billion gallons of ethanol that would be needed for a nationwide gasohol fuels program would, according to Bergland, "tend to lock the nation into allocation of grain feedstock approximating total plant capacity."[12]

Part III

Saving the Land

The Search For New Approaches

11

Finding the Middleground in Farmland Preservation

In the current post-open space era of farmland preservation, with all its strategic implications for the nation, policy makers and plain citizens have been casting about for new approaches for the direct control of farmland, which compared to zoning would have greater promise of being permanent, and compared to the purchase of development rights could be affordable if applied over sizeable areas. The idea is to find something new that could be added to standard techniques, to increase the options for farm communities to protect their land.

What has been sought, in short, is a kind of middleground between zoning (mutable, but cheap) and development rights purchase (permanent, but expensive) which has the best features of both. There are no perfect examples of such a middleground, but there are enough bits and pieces to suggest an important new dimension in land saving. While the bits and pieces are quite variable, there is one feature that seems to be central: the purchase of land as a last resort, when its sale would result in an inappropriate change of use, and its resale with restrictions insuring continued agricultural use. The discussion following examines applications of this idea in Pennsylvania, California, Canada, France, and by private land conservancies in the U.S. who have used purchase and resale extensively for natural area preservation and now are seeking to adapt the approach to farmland.

Pennsylvania Deed Restriction Program

It started out naturally enough. Amish and Mennonite farmers in southeastern Pennsylvania did not want to see land going out of farming and so, cooperatively, bought land so threatened and resold it to people interested in retaining the land in agriculture. Subsequently, and for the past seven years, Amos Funk, a vegetable farmer and conservation leader in Lancaster County, Pennsylvania (the number one ranking non-irrigated agricultural county in the U.S. in terms of the value of products sold), has sought to codify such a notion in his county and in the laws of Pennsylvania. The result is now called the "deed restriction" proposal.[1] The idea is to place a covenant in the deeds over farmland within a duly established agricultural preserve district. The deed restriction is to last 25 years and would preclude inappropriate conversion of the land to other uses. Landowners would have taxes reduced, and be protected from condemnation, nuisance ordinances, and the like. The effort to secure covenants would take place in three "tiers." First, donated covenants would be sought. Then, where donations are not made over land thought to be significant in the district, the agricultural preserve district's board would seek to purchase such covenants based on a percentage of overall land value or for a flat fee per acre. The price offered would be significantly less than traditional "development rights"—permanently deeded negative easements running with the land in perpetuity. For Lancaster County, the figure of $200 per acre was agreed upon for what amounted to a term easement or covenant.

Assuming that not all landowners within the district would think the compensation offered for a 25-year deed restriction sufficient, a third tier could come into play. If and when unrestricted farmland were sold, the board could insert itself into the transaction, if it wished, by exercising a presumptive first option on the land at a purchase price at or in excess of the selling price, and then resell the land with the 25-year restriction placed upon it. This transaction would be voluntary on both sides — the agricultural preserve board would not have to buy the land, the owner would not have to sell it to them. Moreover, the board cannot keep the land, and if it cannot resell it with a restriction, it may sell the land without one if need be.

All of this is complicated but important as an example of a purchase and resale approach. Below is a technical summary prepared for an early draft of the agricultural preserve district bill by the chief counsel of the Pennsylvania House of Representatives: "It [a preliminary draft of the bill] would authorize counties to adopt agricultural preserve ordinances. The ordinances could enable counties to create special agricultural preserve districts. Any time land is sold within a special district, a copy of the contract must be submitted to a newly created agricultural preserve board. The sale of land would have no binding legal effect and could not be recorded for a period of 30 days after the filing of such a contract with the board. The board would be authorized to acquire the purchaser's interest in the land, within this 30-day period, by making a binding, written offer to the seller at a price which *exceeds* the original contract price. Such an acquisition must be approved by a majority of the county commissioners. If the board fails to take any action within this 30-day period, the initial land sale takes effect and cannot be set aside. The board must impose a restrictive covenant upon any land it acquires under this act, limiting it to agricultural [use]. The board must resell the land as restricted. The county is authorized to lease the land until it is resold. The board must first offer the land, at cost, to the initial purchaser, and if rejected, to any person leasing the land. If neither offer is accepted, the board must sell the land at a public sale. The draft [bill] would also enable persons owning land within an agricultural preserve district to voluntarily subject their land to such a restrictive covenant [presumably either by donation or with compensation]. Land voluntarily restricted would be entitled to the same benefits [tax abatement, e.g.] and protections [against condemnation, nuisance ordinances, etc.] as land acquired and resold by the county."[2]

In November 1979 a bill generally conforming to the foregoing description was introduced in the Pennsylvania legislature. The bill—H.B. 1983—failed to be reported out of the Agriculture and Rural Affairs Committee.

While state-level legislation did not succeed, Lancaster County did establish, on its own, a kind of first-step deed restriction program. On April 2, 1980, the county commissioners unanimously passed a measure establishing an agricultural preserve board, permitting voluntary programs to be set up in most of the townships.

The board's mandate is as follows: (1) development of sample deed restrictions; (2) delineation of agricultural preserves, initially and on a continuing basis, in cooperation with the Lancaster County Planning Commission and similar groups; (3) education of the general public, and potential participants, about the deed restrictions program; (4) provision of assistance to those farmland owners who wish to apply deed restrictions; (5) administration of necessary procedures for obtaining re-

strictions; (6) preparation of recommendations for legislation for a more effective deed restriction program; and
(7) expansion of the deed restriction program when and
if new legislation is passed.[3]

The last two points are, of course, crucial if the
central element of the idea—purchase and resale—is to
be realized. But even though this element is missing,
most believe that the county's action to establish a board
is an important step, and should not be thought of merely
as a compromise. "It is very affordable," says Amos
Funk, "and offers, by providing large contiguous areas
designated as preserves, the only real assurance farmers
have to provide for themselves 'the right to farm.' We
certainly have not given up on bill 1983. We will push for
its passage as hard as we can. However, we can wait."[4]

California Coastal Conservancy

One of the most ambitious land use regulation programs
in the United States is administered by the California
Coastal Commission, first authorized by a citizen-led
ballot initiative known as Proposition 20. Proposition 20
was approved by 55 percent of those voting in the general elections of fall, 1972, and it was by all accounts an
amazing demonstration of a shared sense of the value of
an important resource.[5]

The regulatory aspects of the Commission's program
have received most of the attention since—both good
and bad. This involves permit and planning authority
over land within the coastal zone, in some cases severely
limiting its use. Less well-known is a state-level agency
called the State Coastal Conservancy which was established by the legislature four years later, in 1976, to augment the planning and regulatory work of the Commission.[6]

Beginning operations in 1977 with a $7 million budget, the Conservancy has undertaken 39 projects under one or another of its five program areas to: (1) preserve coastal "resource" lands, such as wetlands and habitat areas; (2) redesign unacceptably planned developments, such as the many 40-by-60 foot seaside subdivisions of the 1930s still uncompleted but still "legal," by lot consolidation and resale; (3) provide public access ways to the shore; (4) reserve coastal resource sites through advance acquisition of land for later development as recreation areas by municipalities or state agencies; and (5) preserve agricultural land by acquisition of fee or lesser interest when necessary to restore such lands to productivity.[7]

What distinguishes the Coastal Conservancy is its conscious effort to come up with innovative solutions to its land preservation challenges, using all forms of acquisition and resale or leaseback to achieve its purposes. An example are the projects consolidating lots in badly platted subdivisions by purchasing the unbuilt-upon lots, replatting, and then offering better planned homesites for sale. In the Santa Monica Mountains, one subdivision, El Nido, was reduced from 202 lots to 16 this way. In Seal Beach, the Conservancy developed a public/private investment scheme in which seven percent of the site will pay for 80 percent of the public costs on the remainder of the site. Working with local citizens who established the Humboldt North Coast Land Trust (a private organization set up with the assistance of the Trust for Public Lands), the Conservancy saved the state as much as 34 percent in land costs by judicious advance purchase of lands slated for park use by means of using tax laws creatively to negotiate so-called "bargain sales" from landowners.[8]

Despite these successes the most "monumental" of the Conservancy's mandates, as they describe it, is the preservation of agricultural land, and it seems to be the most elusive. Under the State Coastal Conservancy statute, the Conservancy "may acquire fee title, development rights, easements, or other interests in land located in the coastal zone in order to prevent loss of agricultural land to other uses and to assemble agricultural lands into parcels of adequate size permitting continued agricultural production," and "shall take all feasible action to return to private use or ownership, with appropriate use restrictions, all lands acquired for agricultural preservation. . . ."[9]

Though the instructions are clear, the Conservancy has been unable even to get started on the purchase and resale, or lease, of any of the 3.5 million acres of the state's coastal agricultural lands.[10]

A "model" agricultural land preservation project was to be in the Morro Valley in San Luis Obispo County. The idea was to purchase, in fee, some 146 acres, record an agricultural preservation easement over the land, and transfer the land to an adjoining farmer who would, in turn, place an easement over his own 92-acre property. The scheme would have produced a total of 238 acres permanently preserved as agricultural land. The difficulty was that the Conservancy's appraisal of the value of the land did not meet the owner's expectations and the deal fell through.[11] Though the agency has indirect powers of eminent domain (through the State Public Works Board), condemning the property in order to carry out the plan was apparently not appropriate. Among other things, the Conservancy must get approval from the Coastal Commission before any effort to condemn land, and the commission must, in turn, assure itself that there is "no other reasonable means, including the use of police power, of assuring continuous use of such lands for agricultural purposes." [12]

Subsequently, four other efforts were made to bring off an agricultural purchase and resale, and though one of these is still possible, no projects have yet been completed to preserve agricultural land.

The Conservancy lays the blame not only on the relatively short time it has been in operation, but on extreme budget constraints. Based on its research and field experience, the Conservancy believes that in view of dramatic increases in the development value of coastal land, the resale of purchased land would recoup only fifty cents for each acquisition dollar after imposition of a restrictive easement on the land. Therefore, a fund for purchase and resale would have to be substantial in order to sustain such losses on each purchase and resale transaction. At present, only $1 million is allocated for the farmland program, and, according to the Conservancy, the acquisition budget for most projects—never mind a whole program—would be about $1.5 million each. "Nevertheless," says the Conservancy's report, "because this program is so vitally important, the Conservancy (will) try to demonstrate the efficacy of the program's techniques and potential, given adequate funding." [13]

Canadian Examples

Looking abroad for revealing precedents for domestic policy concepts is usually an effort of a great deal more interest to researchers than to policymakers. With that caveat in mind, it is nevertheless relevant, and possibly even important, to know something about conservancy techniques—if they may now be called that—in two countries, Canada and France. In Canada three provinces—British Columbia, Saskatchewan, and tiny Prince Edward Island—seem to have lessons for the U.S.

In British Columbia, the concept of agricultural districting by means of governmental ukase is almost perfectly demonstrated. In 1972, when the New Democratic Party was elected to form a government for the province, one of the policy priorities was for the protection of farmland from urban encroachment. Accordingly, the NDP government ordered a "freeze" prohibiting the subdivison of farmland, except as ordered to the contrary by the government. Under the 1973 Environment and Land Use Act, the freeze was redefined as pertaining to any parcel of land two acres or more that had been designated as agricultural for property taxation or was in Canadian soil class 1, 2, 3, or 4—meaning good to excellent in terms of soil capability. A Land Commission was empowered to establish permanent Agricultural Land Reserves wherein non-agricultural use of land is prohibited. Such reserves now represent about five percent of the total land area of the province. Appeals for exclusion from the reserves are possible, and as of 1978, about 25,000 acres has been exempted out of the 11.6 million acres in reserve status. In dealing with amendments to review zoning, the basic criterion is agricultural land capability, which indicates how seriously B.C. takes the preservation of its prime farmland.[14]

Germane to the conservancy idea, the province also takes seriously the nature of farmland ownership—the preservation of family farms being second only to the preservation of the land itself in terms of the Land Commission's priorities. One way the Commission helps to encourage small proprietorships is to purchase farms that come on the market and to lease them to young farm families unable to afford the high capital costs of entering the industry as an owner. Fifteen such purchases had been made by the commission as of 1976. Total acreage was just over 6,000, and the cost was $4.4 million including improvements. The long-term lease provides a sense of ownership "just short of outright title," according to one report.[15]

It is Saskatchewan, though, that is best known for its land purchase program to enable young farmers to enter agriculture. The Saskatchewan Land Bank Act of 1972 has been widely reported in the U.S. and has served as inspiration for a "Young Farmers" program in Minnesota and for a 1978 proposal introduced in the U.S. House of Representatives as part of the Family Farm Development Act (H.R. 10716).

The land bank program was established to help solve a number of interrelated farmland ownership and use problems. In rural Saskatchewan, farm areas needed economic revitalization, farmers wishing to sell land could not find qualified buyers, and young or new farmers were unable or unwilling to make the large capital investments required to enter agriculture. As a result, farm ownerships were getting larger and small farms were disappearing. Land was being lost to agriculture, and rural economies were becoming depressed. The objective of the land bank program was to help owners of farmland dispose of their land at a fair price and to help new or young farmers get established in the industry. This was accomplished by purchasing land then leasing it to qualified applicants on a long-term basis with an option to buy after five years if conventional financing could be secured.[16]

As of 1978, some 350 of the program's 2,300 participants had completed five years of leasing and were eligible to purchase their land. During that year the province changed the policy to reduce the amount paid by the buyer. According to a Lands Directorate report, "The land will be sold at the average market price, but purchasers who continue to live and farm in Sasktchewan will be eligible to receive a 20 percent refund (up to $5,000) five years after the purchase. Hence, those persons exercising the purchase option would be those most likely to keep the land in productive agriculture over a long term.[17]

Of all the provincial agricultural land programs, possibly the most interesting for the purposes of this inquiry is one of the least well known—the Prince Edward Island Land Development Corporation, established in 1969. In part, the corporation's job is, like the California Coastal Conservancy's, to augment the regulatory provisions of the province's development plan by means of judiciously buying and selling properties to advance the purposes of the plan.

A major problem in Prince Edward Island, as in British Columbia and Saskatchewan, was the abandonment of small farm holdings —many of them on first rate agricultural land. The corporation can purchase such lands, improve them by repairing structures, installing drain tiles, undertaking erosion control measures, and the like, then resell or lease them on favorable terms to adjoining farmers or other bona fide farmers. In acquiring land, the corporation may buy land outright from an owner. Those owners who are farmers of retirement age may elect to have the corporation set up an annuity program, providing for pensions. Moreover, the farm owners can be eligible for a lifetime lease on existing houses, plus one acre and guaranteed access.[18]

Another element in the province's program is the Rural Development Council, which is a citizen organization that works closely with the Land Development

Corporation and the Land Use Service Centre—an agency which prepares local plans throughout the province. The Rural Development Council organizes meetings to discuss these local plans, obtaining feedback and generally involving citizens in the planning effort. In connection with land acquisition and resale by the Development Corporation, a council staff person is located in the Land Use Service Center to determine those farmers who might be interested in expanding their holdings by purchasing corporation land, and those farmers who might be interested in retiring.[19]

The Land Development Corporation also purchases land proffered to non-resident or alien buyers but not approved for sale by the Lieutenant Governor in Council, who under a 1972 provincial law must approve all such transactions involving 10 acres or more than 330 feet of shoreline. In a 1976 update, the Lieutenant Governor in Council may require a non-resident purchaser whose petition to buy more than 10 acres (or 330 feet of shore frontage) has been approved to enter into an agreement with the Land Use Commission of the province to guarantee the satisfactory use of the land as a condition of the approval.[20]

Taken together, the activities of the Prince Edward Island Land Development Corporation, the Rural Development Council, and the provision in provincial law regulating land sales to non-residents suggest a means by which many interrelated agricultural land use problems can be dealt with creatively, sensitively and comprehensively at the local level.

The French SAFER

Despite the proximity of Canada and some general similarities in settlement patterns and historical land use, the program of a foreign country most significant to a study of conservancy techniques may be the SAFERs of France. As described by Professor Ann Louise Strong of the Department of City and Regional Planning of the University of Pennsylvania, the work of local, nonprofit *Societes d'Amenagement Foncier et d'Etablissement Rural,* which are statutorily empowered with the right to preempt any sale of farmland in their district, is effective "both to assist those who wish to remain in farming to obtain suitable land, and to keep prime land from being subdivided." [21]

The basic operation of a SAFER is relatively straightforward. Authorized in 1960 as non-profit corporations empowered to buy and sell farmland, a SAFER could be established for a single *departement* (county) or for several together. SAFERs now extend to virtually all *departements* in France. The largest covers five *departements.*

Most of the capital for their operation, primarily for a revolving fund, comes from local farm organizations and farm lending institutions. The average start-up capital subscription in 1975 was $200,000.

SAFERs can buy farmland either through voluntary sale or by right of preemption, in previously designated areas. Preemption, which actually is used in only 16 percent of cases, is considered to be essential to the effective operation of the SAFER. Professor Strong describes the process as follows: "The SAFER requests the prefect to designate a given area as subject to the right of preemption for farm use. No land in a development district and no land shown in an adopted plan as intended for urban uses may be included. The prefect must seek the advice of farm organizations concerning the proposed designation and then submits a recommendation to the Minister of Agriculture. If the recommendation is favorable, the

Minister publishes a decree designating the area [as subject to preemption]. The decree is published among the legal notices in newspapers, posted at municipal offices, and mailed to notaries. People selling farm land are deemed to have notice of it, and any sale without prior notice to SAFER is void. The right of preemption is granted for a three to five year term and may be renewed. About 60 percent of agricultural land is subject to a SAFER right of preemption."[22]

Under a voluntary sale of land to a SAFER, the price paid is negotiable. When preemption takes place, the price is set by a public appraisal. Farm organizations in France insisted on the right of preemption coupled with a public appraisal to assure that the SAFER could keep good land in agriculture and avoid a kind of hit or miss performance that might vitiate a preservation program if these authorities were not available.

After acquiring land, the SAFER may make conservation and other improvements before resale. The land may be held for up to five years (under special circumstances, 10) so that a tract-assembly project can be carried out. In France the tradition has been to divide land between heirs rather than devolving it on the eldest son. The result is that in some areas farmland holdings are inappropriately small acreages.

The SAFER resells most of its land to farmers. "The objective is to sell the land not to the highest bidder," writes Professor Strong, "but to the person who will benefit most as a farmer by its acquisition. Favored by the law are farmers with too little land, farmers willing to change their present tracts for more efficient holdings, farmers whose land had been condemned for a public purpose, and young farmers anxious to establish themselves."[23] Significantly, the purchaser must farm the land for a minimum of 15 years. The land may not be sold or subdivided during that period, except in extraordinary circumstances approved by the SAFER.

Altogether, from 1964 to 1975, SAFERs purchased 2.1 million acres of land and sold 1.7 million. They buy an average of only 12 percent of the agricultural land up for sale each year, but most believe that their influence is much greater than the figures would suggest. The key feature is the right of preemption. Even when not used, the possibility of its use can have an important effect on market behavior, an aspect of the device that might be overlooked by those concerned that preemptive purchase is too expensive or too controversial for effective use in the U.S. Says Professor Strong, "Preemption is a power compatible with the American legal system and with American values. There is ample precedent for it in the private market's use of the right of first refusal. Preemption is an approach which, with minor modifications, could be adopted in the U.S. for the purpose of preserving farmland."[24]

Non-Governmental Programs

Real estate activity has become a mainstay land preservation technique for both national and local private conservation organizations in recent years. During the 1960s the Nature Conservancy, with a substantial line of credit guaranteed by the Ford Foundation, began the advance purchase of natural areas for later resale to public agencies such as the National Park Service. Other organizations have used this technique also, including the Western Pennsylvania Conservancy, the Trust for Public Land, and many more. What such institutions could provide was an opportunistic and efficient way to acquire needed land for public use quickly and cheaply—two qualities tending to elude public agencies which must move slowly and carefully in the sensitive matter of land acquisition.

By and large, such private acquisitions for sale to public agencies have been limited to recreational sites, natural areas, and historic places. Since the emergence of national concern about the loss of farmland, some organizations have sought to adapt their expertise in behalf of farmland preservation.

For example, the Trust for Public Lands (TPL), a national land conservation organization based in San Francisco, provides training and technical assistance to agricultural groups and rural communities who wish to establish their own farmland trusts. With TPL's assistance, private agricultural land trusts have been established in communities in Northern California, Colorado and Wyoming. The Trust places special emphasis on the need to insure the existence of economically viable agriculture in areas where private land trusts operate, and on the need for leadership on the part of farmers and ranchers in trust activities. For example, Ralph Grossi, one of the key players in setting up the Marin County (California) Agricultural Land Trust, is a local dairy rancher who was President of the Marin County Farm Bureau at the time. He is now chairman of the Marin Trust, and continues to exercise a strong leadership role in the farm community. In Colorado, the Mesa County Land Conservancy (also set up with TPL assistance) is headed by a local orchardist, Harry Talbott, Jr., who at the time was Chairman of the county Planning Commission.

Probably the first statewide private agricultural land trust was the Montana Land Reliance, which is working with groups of farmland owners in different parts of the state who wish to protect their land through easements, gifts and other devices.

The private agricultural land trust concept has been especially prominent in the western states, where government activities having to do with the land are looked upon with great disfavor. But the trust concept also has its applications elsewhere.

One example is the Lincoln, Massachusetts, Rural Land Foundation. Though Lincoln is a Boston suburb and not a farm community, the Foundation—in effect a consortium of public-spirited investors—has been able to purchase land and "repackage" it, selling off some areas for development and protecting others as open space.[25]

Possibly the first private conservancy established to preserve farmland in association with a state-level program is the Massachusetts Farmland and Conservation Trust. In Massachusetts, a state-wide governmental program to purchase "agricultural preservation restrictions," called APRs, was established in 1977, with an initial $5 million budget to acquire APRs on 19 farm properties in the state, plus another $5 million available from a recent bond issue. Aware that the effectiveness of this state-managed program might be significantly augmented by a parallel private organization, officials of the Nature Conservancy, along with state agency executive and other conservation leaders, helped bring the Massachusetts Farmland and Conservation Trust into being. It began operations in 1980.

According to Davis Cherington, Director of the Trust, the organization is prepared to acquire farm property which has come on the market, using established bank lines of credit. The Trust would then hold the property in its own name, ultimately placing ownership of the development rights (APR) with the State of Massachusetts, the municipality, the local land trust, or a combination of these. The farm could then be re-sold to a qualified buyer at a price which will permit operations as an economically viable farm.

At the request of the Massachusetts Department of Food and Agriculture, the Trust would buy an APR on a specific farm in those instances where the owner could not afford to wait for the department approval process to be completed. Later, the Trust would re-sell the APR to the Department. In cooperation with professional capital management specialists, the Trust would organize tightly controlled private partnerships to acquire key farm properties for which the state lacks a preservation solution. In addition, the Trust would serve as an interstate clearinghouse for information on methods to protect agricultural land. And it can assist local conservation commissions and local land trusts with farmland acquisition and protection projects through real estate negotiation exeprtise, financial loans, and fund-raising assistance.[26]

At the national level, the American Farmland Trust, set up in 1980 in Washington, D.C., has a program designed to demonstrate a variety of free market techniques which can be utilized by non-profit organizations to protect farmland. Such techniques will include acquisition in fee, and purchase of easements or development rights. In some instances, the techniques will be used to develop some land for housing and other purposes while protecting adjacent farmland. The Trust will place special emphasis on preserving unique agricultural lands, as well as projects which would assist minority and limited resource farmers threatened by trends of consolidation. Given the success of private groups in natural area preservation, non-governmental conservancy techniques might well provide a significant capability in certain areas, most especially if activities are designed to be complementary to governmental programs.

12

Towards A Farmland Conservancy Concept

The five mini-case histories recounted in the previous chapter are surely not the only examples of creative new techniques to preserve farmlands. But they do suggest that new farmland protection techniques are rapidly evolving. In the description of these cases, the new middleground approaches have been referred to as "conservancy techniques."[1] So long as this term is not thought to represent any specific kind of organization, public or private, or an overly narrow set of purposes, "conservancy" may be a useful word in conceptualizing a kind of ideal middleground program for saving farmland. What kind of activities, then, would a "farmland conservancy" undertake?

For the sake of argument, a description of the duties of a conservancy might be summarized this way: A farmland conservancy is a local organization operating within a conservancy district coterminous with county or multicounty lines. The conservancy is empowered by state law to buy and sell land or rights in land for the purpose of maintaining prime, unique, and locally important farmland in farm use; to use its lands to retain or increase the numbers of farms in appropriately sized family proprietorships; and on its properties (and others as appropriate) to undertake needed soil and water conservation improvement projects.

The conservancy may acquire land when offered for sale when it believes that the sale will result in a use inimical to farming, farmland, and conservation values in its area. It may resell the land with restrictions on use to an appropriate buyer, or it may lease land. It may also resell land (when appropriate) for intensive development.

If there is a dispute over the price of land, the price offered shall be based on independent appraisals, or determined by a court in a condemnation proceeding. The conservancy has the right to intervene in any sale of land previously designated by the conservancy as prime, unique, or locally important farmland. The conservancy may use a wide variety of real estate transactions to pursue its purposes, including trades of land or rights in land, payment through pensions or annuities, and the like. It may assemble tracts of land for efficient farm use, or subdivide large tracts into smaller units appropriate to family farming or for young farmers.

If the conservancy has undertaken extensive conservation projects on land it has acquired, it may stipulate in the deed upon resale that the conservation improvements be maintained, enforceable by right of reverter. In the area of its operations, the conservancy will cooperate with other government authorities, encouraging them to plan, regulate, tax and otherwise control land use in the agricultural area in such a way as to stabilize and enhance farming as an enterprise and way of life.

Approaches to Organization

For a concept such as the foregoing to be adopted, any number of different kinds of institutions might be able to carry out the program—including agencies of local government, agencies of state government, special districts (especially conservation districts), or private organizations with public charter—assuming proper legislative authority.

The Lancaster Agricultural Preserve Board is an example of an agency of general purpose local government. It was created by the county commissioners as, in effect, a committee. This status gives the board access to the powers of the local government, and vice versa. Though the board does not yet have its sought-after deed restriction authority, if this element is added to the program the work of the board can be coordinated with other authorities held by local government—including zoning, taxing, and eminent domain. There are some who believe that it might be improper for the same government that depresses the value of land through regulation to turn around and buy the land at the reduced price to accomplish the same general purposes as the regulation. This would be especially improper, some think, if condemnation is used, or even if condemnation is threatened directly or indirectly. This is one of the reasons why the Coastal Commission in California was set up as a separate organization from the Coastal Conservancy.

While the Coastal Conservancy does not have the problem of zoning land and acquiring it too, there are other difficulties with it as a model. The main problem is that the California Conservancy is *un*local and does not operate within any kind of predetermined area in which farmland values are specifically identified. This should not be interpreted as a criticism of the Conservancy, for its program is comprehensive and not limited to agricultural land. Still, there are, probably, better models for state-level agencies taking on the role of a farmland conservancy—possibly localized state park authorities could be looked to for guidance. Conceivably, there could be a state-level farmland conservancy operated on a farm district basis with local operations in each cooperating district. This would effectively separate the program from general purpose local government, but perhaps be a bit more bureaucratic than necessary.

Special districts are a traditional means to provide for special programs. School districts are the most prevalent case in point, but in many areas, special districts provide most services, and farmland conservancy activities need not be an exception. It is entirely conceivable that state enabling legislation could be enacted which would provide sufficient statutory authority for a local conservancy district to be established, drawing funds and its general powers from the state level of government. In this connection, there is already in existence a special district program associated with agricultural land that is represented in virtually all farm areas of the U.S. The reference is to the Soil and Water Conservation Districts, set up under a model state enabling act sent to state governments in 1937 by President Franklin Delano Roosevelt. Conservation districts duly established under suitable state law are eligible for soil and water conservation grants and technical assistance from the U.S. Department of Agriculture and other agencies. The standard state law provides a procedure, including a local petition and referendum, for the organization of soil conservation districts as governmental subdivisions of the state, but governed by a local board of supervisors. A state-level committee administers the procedures establishing the districts, and provides administrative assistance and coordination of programs.

What is significant in terms of conservation districts is that some of them might be able to undertake most farmland conservancy techniques as they have been described here with little if any change in their charters. There are nearly 3,000 conservation districts with a total of 17,000 people serving as district officials. Some 775 districts—or 41 percent of those responding to a 1979 survey—have already expressed concern about the loss of agricultural land to urban development. In some areas, conservation districts have led the way in urging local farmland protection ordinances. In others, they are not so effective.

Lastly, it is possible that private organizations might have a direct as well as complementary role in conservancy-type activities. It is possible that state governments could charter existing private organizations—such as land trusts in New England towns—to undertake expanded programs for landsaving and be empowered to use or "borrow" authorities necessary to carry out such programs. Without the authority to preempt land sales or to protect against profiteering by private landsellers, however, private groups would be limited to a kind of "augmenting" role, such as that described for the Massachusetts Farmland and Conservation Trust.

There are—without question—some serious issues to be resolved concerning any theorized farmland conservancy program. Several stand out: the problems of money and equity, the problem of administrative sufficiency and unintended effects, and the problem of politics.

The Problems of Funding and Equity

The money issue has several parts, the most important being the amount of money needed up front for a revolving fund, and the amount of money needed to replenish the fund, assuming that stripping development rights from land titles would lower the price considerably in some areas. With farmland prices averaging $1,500 per acre in the Northeast and the Cornbelt, the acquisition of a single 250 acre farm in these areas would run $375,000. According to Coastal Conservancy calculations, one should expect to lose 50 percent (i.e., $750 when the average farmland price is $1,500 per acre) on a turn-around transaction after taking out development value. Thus, the net cost for "processing" a 250-acre farm would be $187,500, not counting overhead or cost of improvement of the property. Using SAFER figures, where *departement* capitalization averaged $200,000 (half a million today?), one farm turnover would be enough to break the budget. But this manner of figuring may be excessively negative. To begin with, only three percent of farm properties turn over in a given year. And of those only a small fraction are to non-farm buyers. And of *those*, not all sales would necessarily relate to preservation of prime land. Therefore, only a small percentage of farms in the average conservancy districts would be up for sale, and only a fraction of those would require intervention. Moreover, if the French experience is any guide, inappropriate sales would probably be suppressed by the very existence of a conservancy-type institution. One last observation: With the cost of land escalating at present rates—ranging up to 25 percent per year—the chances are that some conservancies might well recoup their investment, even after stripping development rights from the title (provided they also had the ability to sell some land for intense development purposes as the California Coastal Conservancy is authorized to do). Given the foregoing rough arithmetic, money would be a problem, but not invariably so. In fact, in areas of high turnover, funding might even be more manageable than in other areas simply because land which the conservancy sold for development could offset the cost of land purchased for preservation.

As for issues of equity, this concerns "fairness." On the one hand, is it fair to farmland owners in a conservancy district to have their property subjected to special rules and regulations that inhibit their freedom to sell property to whomever they wish? And on the other hand is it fair to the taxpayer to be asked to subsidize, in effect,

the farm sector by having to insure that farmland is not misused? These are serious questions—and not the only ones bearing on equity issues, either—that pertain to conservancy techniques. However, in theory at least, it would appear that the conservancy approach might better avoid some of the equity difficulties as compared to the use of police power without compensation, or the use of tax revenues for the large scale purchase of development rights.

Administration and Unintended Effects

The problem of administrative sufficiency has several aspects. First, can a local body be expected to undertake what amounts to quite sophisticated land transactions? Won't problems of loopholes, favoritism, or just plain administrative stupidity creep in? The SAFERs of France—a program with enough time in operation to provide a benchmark—are heavily criticized for various operational failures. At the same time, the program is still in effect, and while not perfect, most believe that the French agricultural land base has benefitted enormously by virtue of the program, possibly in ways that are difficult to measure. Moreover, the U.S. agricultural community is, in most areas, well organized, with enough institutional and agency programs in operation, that much administrative capability is already in place.

These days, official Washington, as well as many state capitals are more concerned about the unintended effects of new government programs. Indeed, it is almost mandatory to mention in any analysis of land use policy that government programs are often a part of the problem rather than part of the solution. Could this be true of an organized farmland conservancy program? The fact is that an aggressive operation could, by intervening vigorously in the land market, distort prices. What is worse, it might be that a future generation will find that the wrong land has been preserved. In some instances, no doubt, areas that might have been best used for urban expansion, say, might be those protected as farmland. There are some quite technical problems too. What, for example, should a conservancy program imply for agricultural zoning? Would such zoning be superfluous in an area where farmland is subject to preemptive purchase and resale with deeded restrictions? And if this is true, could conservancies ultimately be subversive of the long and difficult efforts many farm counties have made to achieve farm-use zoning? There is hardly any way to answer these questions, except possibly to place the issue of potential unintended effects stemming from farmland conservancies against the effects stemming from zoning and/or development rights purchase—or simple tax abatement for that matter. In every case, government intervention into the market mechanism has, and will have, the possibility of creating as well as solving problems.

And Politics

This last point leads into the problem of *politics*. Any kind of intervention in land use is difficult to sell in the United States, and most difficult in rural areas where a laissez faire attitude about land use has been a long tradition. Conservancy techniques, while perhaps more in "the American grain" than some kinds of zoning, are easily misunderstood, especially when coupled with the right of preemption and back-up powers of eminent domain to settle problems of compensation. A new idea is always hard to introduce. It is harder usually in rural areas than in urban ones. And if the idea has something to do with "land use" there are those who wouldn't even consider trying.

What then are the options? New approaches to farmland preservation such as those discussed do not have to be introduced tomorrow. Instead, what really faces policymakers is the need to develop a certain kind of intellectual *stance* with regard to farmland preservation—one which is open to new ideas and willing to experiment. The set of techniques presented here is thought to be worthy of serious consideration because it deals with interrelated aspects of farmland ownership and use: it combines the conversion issue, the family-farm/tenure issue, and the resource conservation issue into one set of considerations. These problems are not all that's awry with farming these days, but they do go to the very heart of U.S. agriculture policy, and hence to basic domestic and international issues facing our nation.

13

Farmland and the Future

When the early warnings of a coming cropland squeeze were first brought forth by the Soil Conservation Service a half decade ago, few foresaw how quickly the farmland protection issue would emerge from obscurity. In fact, at a time when U.S. agriculture appears to be more productive than it has ever been before, the response has been little short of remarkable.

And yet, it is well to remember just what has been accomplished to date. Despite all the state and local activity, less than 20 million acres (according to the National Agricultual Lands Study) is covered by a farmland protection program worthy of the mention. Among the major farm states, only one, Wisconsin, has a statewide program to protect farmland. As for the federal government, only two agencies—the Department of Agriculture and the Environmental Protection Agency—have adopted policies to scrutinize their own activities in terms of their impacts on farmland. And the Congress itself has been unwilling to adopt even the most modest legislation to help states and localities deal with the problem.

Breaking New Ground

If the accomplishments have been encouraging but
small, the problem itself is discouragingly large. It can be
summarized as follows: At a time when every available
acre is being pressed into crop production, the U.S. is
losing a great deal more cropland, and has a great deal
less cropland in reserve than anyone previously thought.
Barring the extremes of a collapse in world demand, on
the one hand, or a truly revolutionary breakthrough in
agricultural technology on the other, we have entered an
era in which the limits of the land will establish the
productive capacity of U.S. agriculture as surely as have
yields per acre in the past. For U.S. agriculture is now
driven by a world dynamic of demand that is forcing
farmers to bring more land into cultivation even though
yields may increase.

This is the new reality that lies behind the projection by the National Agricultural Land Study that U.S.
farmers may need to bring between 77 and 113 million
additional acres into cultivation by the year 2000.
Whether one chooses to accept the low figure (based on
extremely optimistic assumptions about yield improvement) or the high figure (based on how yields actually
behaved over the last decade) is immaterial: in either
case, farmers will have to break new ground to accommodate whatever expansion does occur because cultivation of the existing cropland base of 413 million acres has
now reached its practical limits.

As to this "new ground" on which such an expansion
might occur, it, too, is far more limited than was once
thought. A decade ago, those who might worry about
whether there would be enough farmland in the future
could be reassured to the contrary by a USDA estimate

that the country had 266 million acres of "cropland in reserve" that could be tapped if the need arose. That figure has not withstood scrutiny. For, when actual costs to the farmer are factored in, less than half of this land (127 million acres) has even a medium potential to be brought into production, and of this only 36 million acres has a high potential.

Even here, economic tradeoffs will be required to bring this land into production. The reservoir of potential cropland is in no sense vacant or idle acreage. Most of it is already committed to pasture, range and woodland uses which would be displaced or discontinued if cultivation were to begin. Moreover, cultivation on much of this land would result in erosion problems unless costly conservation practices are adopted.

Under the best of circumstances, then, *only about 12 percent of the agricultural land not presently in cultivation can be pressed into service to make up for urbanization and other development of existing cropland.* Significantly, this attenuated cropland reserve is itself made up of land especially vulnerable to urbanization since it is fairly level, easy to build on, and is often located in areas of benign climate.

It is against the reality of a more limited land base and an intensified demand for agricultural products that the loss of farmland to other uses must be judged. In this regard, it would be a mistake to construc too narrowly the statistics on land conversion as the measure of urbanization's real impact on agriculture. The most commonly cited statistic, which asserts that development takes three million acres of farmland each year (one third of which is cropland), is in itself a sobering reflection of the magnitude of the problem, for this is roughly three times the rate that farmland conversion was estimated to be occurring a decade ago. Even more sobering, this figure does not take into account the indirect effects on farming, as land begins to be idled in advance of development.

Just how great those effects might be is only now beginning to be grasped, for the monumental downward shift in "land in farms" that NALS was able to derive from the Census of Agriculture is almost certainly a reliable barometer of the "impermanence syndrome." The 88 million acre decline that occurred between 1969 and 1978—an average of 9.8 million acres per year—was not picked up early enough by NALS for its full implications to be assessed, but it has given pause even to those most skeptical about the need to protect farmland from indiscriminate development.

Will these trends continue? Most likely, yes— unless resolute action is taken to direct new development away from high quality farmland. The current reduction in new housing starts is not a meaningful measure of the demand which a still growing population is likely to exert in the years to come. For the peak of the demand for new housing by the baby-boom generation will not be reached until the early 1990s, and even then it will taper off in a bell-shaped curve.

Rural Urbanization

Moreover, the confirmation by the 1980 population Census of the "turnaround" in rural population trends first picked up by USDA demographers in the mid-1970s suggests that the edge between rural and urban land uses will become even more blurred in the future.

Instead of a declining rural population in favor of growing urban centers, census figures now show that rural areas are increasing their population and that it is increasing far faster than cities or their suburbs. This is not a failure in the definition of what a city really is, for even counties that themselves are not adjacent to metropolitan areas are growing faster than counties within metropolitan areas. To be sure, metropolitan areas are still gaining more people in absolute numbers, but the urbanization of farmland and its ripple effects for farm communities, are no longer phenomena limited to the fringes of large cities.

The statistical evidence of non-metropolitan growth is underscored by the visual evidence. Increasingly, rural America is scarcely distinguishable from suburban America. Sprawl is now a pervasive pattern of development everywhere; and it leads to a weakening of the highly specialized and therefore fragile agriculturally-oriented rural economy and family-farm ownership structure.

U.S. agriculture is celebrated as the most productive in the world, based in large part on the fact that it is an economically decentralized proprietary enterprise. It is still possible to describe this enterprise as "family farming." And there is a good case to be made that the agricultural land problem derives from the same set of factors as the family farm problem—that is, the increasingly rapid disappearance of such farms as the mainstay of U.S. agriculture. It is truly said that there is no value in preserving the resource base without preserving the economic activity which sustains it. Therefore, if the U.S. resource base is in trouble, it is because the resource users—family farms—are in even worse trouble.

What lies at the heart of both the family farm problem and the urbanization problem may be the land *price* problem. As described earlier in this book, through the 1970s, the price of farmland increased at a rate two and one half times that of inflation. An important reason for this is that farmland is an attractive sheltered investment for urban-industrial wealth. The flow of investment dollars into farmland has been encouraged by favorable tax laws and exacerbated by fear of inflation. The result? Farmland is in the process of being priced out of the market for farm use. Discontinuous urban development, far from metropolitan areas, is both a cause and effect in this equation. The capability of land to be sold for development *somewhere,* suggests to each and all that land can be sold for development *anywhere.* Therefore the prices go up *everywhere,* making the marketing of land for non-agricultural use increasingly difficult to resist. The effect of all this is to make paper millionaires out of some farmers and to provide others with mortgagable value to borrow against in order to afford high-cost machinery. But there is another effect—to preclude the non-established farmer from full participation in agriculture because the price of farmland is just too high.

Logic would require that if small or medium size farmers cannot enter or fully participate in the business of farming, it is only a matter of time until there are no proprietary farmers farming at all. This is, for most, a nightmarish vision of vertical integration, super-agribusiness, and absentee ownership carried to the final degree. The nightmare will not be analyzed here, but it is safe to say that the concomittant trends toward larger and fewer farms that were so clearly documented in USDA's structure study are wholly implicated—and may well have a controlling role—in the kind of agricultural future the United States will have.

This is no frivolous matter in a country which has discovered, once again, that it is an "agricultural nation." One need only take a look at the foreign trade figures of the U.S. for recent years to ascertain the re-ascendency of agriculture in the national economy. After increasing slowly in the 1950s and '60s, food export income doubled in the 1970s, then doubled again twice. The year just passed, 1980, holds the record: $40.5 billion worth of food sold abroad—the largest single component of our export trade.

Most agree—and we are among them—that this phenomenal economic achievement is a reflection of strength in our agricultural system. But assessed against this undeniable success are some real costs. The fact that 140 million acres of crop land are eroding at rates beyond the capacity for natural replenishment of the soil; the suspicion that the trend towards farm enlargement may already or soon will pass the threshold size necessary for optimal farm efficiency; and indeed the pressures to run the land at full throttle—all point to systemic problems within industrial agriculture as currently practiced in the U.S.

Because the ecology of agriculture is not endlessly elastic, the additional stress created by non-agricultural development of the land base threatens permanently to reduce the productive capacity of American agriculture. It is possible to substitute fertilizer for land, unless, of course, the next increment of fertilizer costs more than the increased yield will bring in prices. It is possible to substitute pesticides for land, unless it costs more to kill the pests than to lose the crop they destroy. It is possible to substitute water for land, diesel fuel for land, new genetic stocks for land—all of these, but only up to a point.

This is why the efforts of states and counties to protect their farmland resources can no longer be viewed as isolated responses to purely local problems, irrelevant as a whole to agriculture. To the contrary, the rapid expansion of such efforts is urgent and crucial to the national interest.

One simple way to express the national interest is to

"put the federal house in order." There is a clear and compelling case for an overall federal policy which would keep federal programs from causing the loss of farmland. Farmland retention would no doubt be encouraged if the federal government were to stop creating urban investment opportunities by putting roads, sewers, and other urban amenities into important farm areas.

Another way the federal government could avoid being part of the problem would be to remove the income tax advantages of speculating in farmland. The Internal Revenue Code is thought to have a considerable influence on both the structure of agriculture and dispersed urban growth patterns which needlessly consume good farmland. There are at least 24 sections of the code that directly affect real estate, and there are many more that have an indirect effect on land use.[1] Code policies have been implicated in, among many other things, the decline of inner cities and the spread of suburban sprawl; in the purchase of raw farmland by non-farm investors; in the trend towards larger and larger farms; and, through the federal estate tax, in the premature conversion of farm real estate by heirs simply to pay off the inheritance tax. The Congress adjusted the estate tax provisions in 1976, 1978 and again in 1981 to ease the impact of the inheritance tax on heirs willing to keep farmland in farm use, but further adjustments are needed.[2]

Given the current interest in tax reform, and in distortions of the economy caused by federal policies, it might be that now is the time to begin assessment of the IRS Code and its implications for land use. The tax code permits an enormous "tax expenditure" pertaining to land use—i.e., loss of tax revenues to the federal government that would be paid were it not for the land-related

tax shelters. Land related tax expenditures may total up-
wards of $50 billion *per year* according to one aggrega-
tion.[3]

But tinkering with the IRS code, and tidying up
federal programs are not by themselves a dynamic
enough response to protect farms and farmland—given
contemporary pressures on the land base. Such actions
are essentially passive, at a time when the national interest demands action. That states and localities are now
beginning to move on their own accord suggests that
comprehensive and concrete federal programs to protect
farms and farmland is an urgent priority for the Congress.
Financial and technical support for the kind of innovative approaches discussed in Chapters 11 and 12 of this
book would provide a good starting point.

Obviously, the federal government is wholly implicated in the enterprise of American agriculture, and has
been for half a century, if not longer. The way this relationship is to be extended to cover the protection of the
land-base itself is a question, at this point, that seems to
be a matter of how and when rather than whether. There
are, USDA statisticians say, only 36 million acres of first
rate land left in the high potential cropland reserve over
and above the land already in use. Of the privately-
owned land in the U.S. that's just two percent—a figure
so astonishingly low, when compared to the vastness of
a continent still not fully explored only a century ago,
that not even the Congress can ignore it with impunity.

Notes

Chapter 1. The Cropland Squeeze

1   U.S. Senate Committee on Interior and Insular Affairs, *Report to Accompany S. 268, Land Use Policy and Planning Assistance Act* (Washington, D.C.: GPO, 1973), pp. 36-37. Although passed twice by the Senate, the House failed to adopt the measure.

2   As defined by the U.S. National Agricultural Lands Study, "agricultural lands" are "lands currently used to produce agricultural commodities including forest products, or lands that have a potential for such production." Under this definition, there were about 1.361 billion acres of agricultural land in 1977. About 590 million acres of this agricultural land may be useful for range, pasture and forestry, but is thought to have no potential for growing cultivated crops. About 413 million acres were considered to be in existing crop use in 1977, while another 127 million acres was considered to have a high or medium potential for growing crops on a regular basis if the need arose.

3   U.S. Department of Agriculture, *Our Land and Water Resources: Current and Prospective Supplies and Uses* (Washington, D.C.: GPO, 1974), pp. vi-viii. The 333 million acre figure for cropland planted encompasses all land planted in crops, including cultivated summer fallow and acreage not harvested due to crop failure. Actual land planted in principal crops was 291 million acres in 1969, of which 280 million was harvested. An additional 8 million acres was devoted to field seeds, commercial vegetables, fruits and planted nuts in 1969.

4 Raymond I. Dideriksen, Allen R. Hidlebaugh, and Keith O. Schmude, *Potential Cropland Study,* U.S. Department of Agriculture Soil Conservation Service Statistical Bulletin No. 578 (Washington D.C.: GPO, 1977).

5 Calvin Beale, U.S. Department of Agriculture, "Internal Migration in the United States since 1970." Hearings before the Select Committee on Population, Feb. 8, 1978. p. 2.

6 The NALS, in addition to its final report, produced five interim reports on specific agricultural land issues, 16 technical papers, 17 reports on NALS regional workshops, a bibliographic source book, and a reference guidebook for state and local governments, entitled *Protecting Farmland.* For most readers, the final report and the guidebook for state and local governments will be the most useful items.

7 U.S. National Agricultural Lands Study, *Final Report* (Washington, D.C.: GPO, 1981), p. 17.

8 For an interesting discussion about the politics surrounding the "Land in Farms" controversy, as well as the NALS in general, see Kenneth A. Cook, "The National Agricultural Lands Study Goes Out With A Bang," *Journal of Soil and Water Conservation* (March-April 1981), pp. 91-93.

9 Block's remarks were prepared for the National Agricultural Lands Conference, held in Chicago in February, 1981.

10 As quoted in Charles E. Little, "The Demise of the Jeffords Bill," *Journal of Soil and Water Conservation* (March-April 1980), p. 99.

Chapter 2. The Beginnings of Farmsaving

1 For a detailed discussion of differential assessment, see John C. Keene, et. al., *Untaxing Open Space: An Evaluation of the Effectiveness of Differential Assessment of Form and Open Space,* Prepared for the U.S. Council on Environmental Quality by the Regional Science Research Institute (Washington, D.C.: GPO, 1976).

2 Robert E. Coughlin, John C. Keene, et al. *The Protection of Farmland: A Reference Guidebook for State and Local Governments.* Prepared for the U.S. National Agricultural Lands Study (Washington, D.C.: GPO, 1981), p. 60.

3   Ibid., p. 220.

4   Ibid., p. 219.

5   Ibid., p. 21.

6   Ibid., p. 87.

7   Ibid.

8   Ibid., p. 194-195. Other factors, too, have played a roll, including declining school enrollments, tight mortgage money, and gas lines.

Chapter 3.   Zoning for Food

1   Robert E. Coughlin, personal communication.

2   The information on Stephenson County is derived from W. Wendell Fletcher, Charles E. Little, et al., *Land Impacts of Rural Population Growth*, An American Land Forum Report (Washington, D.C.: U.S. Council on Environmental Quality, 1980), p. 16.

3   Ibid., p. 33.

4   National Association of Conservation Districts, *The Conversion of Agricultural Land, A Preliminary Report* (Washington, D.C.: National Association of Conservation Districts, 1979), p. 4.

5   Robert Coughlin, personal communication.

6   Ibid.

7   The information on southwestern Oregon is derived from *Land Impacts of Rural Population Growth*.

8   Ibid., p. 69.

9   Ibid., p. 79.

10 Richard P. Benner, "Oregon Farmland Update," *American Land Forum Magazine* (Autumn 1980), p. 6.

11 Ronald Eber, personal communication.

Chapter 4.   Sharing Ownership

1   Information derived from Robert C. Coughlin and John C. Keene, et. al, *The Protection of Farmland: A Reference Guide for State and Local Governments* prepared for the U.S. National Agricultural Lands Study (Washington, D.C.: GPO, 1981), Tables 1.5, and 7.1 and 7.2.

2   Ibid., p. 152.

3   Ibid.

4   See *The Protection of Farmland*, pp. 210-220 for a discussion.

5   Dennis A. White, personal communication.

6   Maryland-National Capital Park and Planning Commission, *Functional Master Plan for the Preservation of Agriculture and Open Space in Montgomery County: Preliminary Plan* (Silver Spring, Maryland: National Capital Park and Planning Commission, 1980), p. 40.

7   *The Protection of Farmland*, p. 17.

Chapter 5.   The Politics of Preservation

1   Charles E. Little, ed., *Land and Food: The Preservation of U.S. Farmland* (Washington, D.C.: American Land Forum, 1979), p. 31. This passage, and some others appearing in this chapter, are from a background paper for an ALF policy forum on cropland conversion (December 1978) prepared by Stanley D. Schiff, an economist and former head of the U.S. Delegation to the U.N. Habitat Conference.

2   See Chapter 2 for a discussion of these failings.

3   U.S. Department of Agriculture, *Recommendations on Prime Lands* (Washington, D.C.: Soil Conservation Service, 1978), p. 12.

4   U.S. National Agricultural Lands Study, *Final Report* (Washington, D.C.: GPO, 1981), p. 85.

5   Report of the Blueprint Commission on the future of New Jersey Agriculture (Trenton: 1973), p. 18.

6   U.S. Department of Agriculture, *A Time to Choose: Summary Report on the Structure of Agriculture* (Washington, D.C.: GPO, 1981), p. 10.

7   Ibid., p. 142.

8   Ibid.

9   Ibid., p. 6.

Chapter 6.   The Global Context

1.   U.S. Department of Agriculture, *A Time to Choose: Summary Report on the Structure of Agriculture* (Washington, D.C.: GPO, 1981), p. 24. The structure study, addressing such topics as farm size, landownership trends, and how the food system meets public objectives, complements the effort of the National Agricultural Lands Study, and should be of key interest to readers concerned about the overall direction of U.S. farm policy.

2   Information provided by USDA Economics Research Service. Because additional acreage each year is devoted to cultivated summer fallow and cropland pasture uses, the 1980 figure approximates full utilization.

3   As quoted in Charles E. Little, ed., *Land and Food: The Preservation of U.S. Farmland* (Washington, D.C.: American Land Forum, 1979), p. 26.

4   U.S. National Agricultural Lands Study, *Final Report* (Washington, D.C.: GPO, 1981), p. 55.

5   *A Time to Choose*, p. 25.

6   Sandra S. Batie and Robert G. Healy, "U.S. Agriculture as a Strategic Resource: The Past and the Future" in *The Future of American Agriculture as a Strategic Resource* (Washington, D.C.: Conservation Foundation, 1980), Ch. 1, p. 15.

7   Presidential Commission on World Hunger, *Overcoming World Hunger: The Challenge Ahead* (Washington, D.C.: GPO, 1980), p. 8.

8   U.S. Interagency Task Force on Tropical Forests, *The World's Tropical Forests: A Policy, Program and Strategy for the United*

States, Department of State Publication 1997 (Washington, D.C.: GPO, 1980), p. 15.

9   As reported in the *Journal of Soil and Water Conservation* (March-April 1981), p. 97.

Chapter 7.   Is There Land Enough?

1   U.S. National Agricultural Lands Study, *Final Report* (Washington, D.C.: GPO, 1981), p. 8.

2   As quoted in the *Journal of Soil and Water Conservation* (March-April 1981), p. 63.

3   Ibid.

4   H. Thomas Frey, *Major Uses of Land in the United States: 1974*, U.S. Department of Agriculture Economic Report No. 440 (Washington, D.C.: GPO, 1979), p. 18.

5   As quoted in Charles E. Little, ed., *Land and Food: The Preservation of U.S. Farmland* (Washington, D.C.: American Land Forum, 1979), p. 16.

6   *Final Report*, p. 50.

7   Ibid., p. 37.

8   As reported in Kenneth A. Cook, "The National Agricultural Lands Study Goes Out With a Bang," *Journal of Soil and Water Conservation* (March-April 1981), p. 92.

9   As quoted in *Journal of Soil and Water Conservation* (March-April 1981), p. 64.

10   *Final Report*, p. 51.

11   John F. Jones, "Farm Real Estate Markets Development," (Washington, D.C.: USDA, May 1980), p. 3.

12   George Perkins Marsh, *The Earth as Modified by Human Action* (New York: Scribner, Armstrong and Company, 1877), p. 48.

13   Arthur M. Schlesinger, *The Coming of the New Deal* (Boston: Houghton Mifflin, 1959), pp. 335-336.

14   As quoted in M. Mitchell Waldrop, "Deep Changes Taking Root in U.S. Agriculture," *Chemical and Engineering News,* June 1, 1981, p. 28.

15   Ibid.

16   National Association of Conservation Districts, *Soil Degradation: Effects on Agricultural Productivity* (Washington, D.C.: U.S. NALS, 1980), p. 93.

17   As quoted in *Journal of Soil and Water Conservation* (March-April, 1981), p. 93.

18   Ibid.

19   "The National Agricultural Lands Study: An Interview with Robert J. Gray," *Journal of Soil and Water Conservation* (March-April 1981), p. 63.

Chapter 8   Productivity and the Ecology of Agriculture

1   As quoted in Charles E. Little, ed., *Land and Food: The Preservation of U.S. Farmland* (Washington, D.C.: American Land Forum, 1979), p. 23.

2   U.S. National Agricultural Lands Study, *Final Report* (Washington, D.C.: GPO, 1981), p. 56.

3   As quoted in *Land and Food,* p. 24.

4   U.S. Department of Agriculture, *A Time to Choose: Summary Report on the Structure of Agriculture* (Washington, D.C.: GPO, 1981), p. 57.

5   *Final Report,* p. 58.

6   R. H. Shaw, "Climate Change and the Future of American Agriculture as a Strategic Resource," in *The Future of American Agriculture as a Strategic Resource* (Washington, D.C.: Conservation Foundation, 1980), Chapter 8, p. 11.

7   Ibid., Chapter 8, p. 49.

8   Lester R. Brown, *By Bread Alone* (New York: Praeger, 1974), p. 118.

9   U.S. Council on Environmental Quality, *Eleventh Annual Report* (Washington, D.C.: GPO, 1980), pp. 359-360.

10   Ibid.

11   See James Ridgeway with Carolyn S. Projons, *Energy-Efficient Community Planning: A Guide to Saving Energy and Producing Power at the Local Level* (Emmaus, Pa.: J. G. Press, no date) for a discussion of the Northglenn approach.

12   U.S. Department of Energy, *National Energy Plan-II: Environmental Trends and Impacts Appendix*, May, 1979, p. 1-36.

13   *Eleventh Annual Report*, p. 348.

14   John S. Steinhart and Carol E. Steinhart, "Energy Use in the U.S. Food System," *Science*, April 19, 1974, p. 311.

15   Wilson Clark, *Energy for Survival: The Alternative to Extinction* (New York: Anchor, 1974), p. 170.

16   Quoted in Richard Merrill, ed., *Radical Agriculture* (New York: Harper Colophon, 1976), p. 79.

17   In Dudley Lynch, "Letter from Pecos: Losing Land to Energy Costs," *Business Week*, 4 October 1976, pp. 20E-20F.

18   As quoted in M. Mitchell Waldrop, "Deep Changes Taking Root in U.S. Agriculture," *Chemical and Engineering News*, June 1, 1981, p. 24.

19   Theo F. Moriak, "Implications of Energy and Environment Upon Growth in the Food and Fiber Sector," *American Journal of Agricultural Economics*, December, 1975, p. 820.

20   Garrison Wilkes, "Plant Germplasm Resources," *Environmental Review* (Spring, 1976), p. 10.

21   *Ibid.*, p. 11-12.

22   R. Neil Sampson, *Farmland or Wasteland* (Emmaus, Pa.: Rodale Press, 1981), p. 236.

23   "Deep Changes Taking Root in U.S. Agriculture," p. 24.

24   See Luther J. Carter, "Organic Farming Becomes 'Legitimate'," *Science*, July 11, 1980, pp. 156-254, for a discussion.

25   Peter S. Carlson and Caroline G. Hoisington, "The New Genetics: Notes from Demeter's Workshop," *The Antioch Review* (Fall 1980), p. 412.

26 John C. Jeavons, "Resource-Conserving Agriculture Method Promises High Yields," Palo Alto, Calif.: Ecology Action of the Mid-Peninsula, January 12, 1976.

27 Hiroshi Johno, "A Solution to Food Problems," *Oriental Economist*, February 1977, pp. 34-35.

Chapter 9. The Energy Overlay

1 Barry M. Casper and Paul David Wellstone, *Powerline: The First Battle in America's Energy War* (Amherst, Mass.: University of Massachusetts Press, 1981).

2 U.S. Department of Interior Bureau of Mines, *Projects to Expand Fuel Sources in Eastern States*, Information Circular 8765 (Washington, D.C.: GPO, 1978) and *Projects to Expand Fuel Sources in Western States*, Information circular 8719 (Washington, D.C.: GPO 1977).

3 As derived from: U.S. Federal Energy Administration, *Project Independence Report*, November, 1974, pp. 213-214, and U.S. Energy Research and Development Administration, *Annual Environmental Analysis Report, 1977*, as reproduced in *Environmental Challenges of the President's Energy Plan*, U.S. House of Representatives Committee on Science and Technology (Washington, D.C.: GPO, 1977), pp. 134-136.

4 U.S. Department of Interior Office of Surface Mining Reclamation and Enforcement, *Final Environmental Impact Statement: Section 501(b) Regulations* (Washington, D.C.: GPO, 1979), p. 13 III-1.

5 U.S. Environmental Protection Agency, *Energy From the West: Policy Analysis Report* (Springfield, Va.: NTIS, 1979), p. 331.

6 Northern Great Plains Resources Program, *Effects of Land Development in the Northern Great Plains*, p. 56.

7 U.S. Department of Agriculture, Resources of the Interior Region and Coal Development, Working Paper #58 (Draft Manuscript), August 1978, p. 81.

8 *Christian Science Monitor*, November 5, 1980, p. 5.

9 See "Reclaiming Mined Land in Illinois for Row Crop Production," by Allen F. Grant, *Journal of Soil and Water Conservation*,

Sept.-Oct., 1978 and *Strip Mining in the Corn Belt,* by John C. Doyle, Jr. (Washington, D.C.: Environmental Policy Institute, 1976) for two different views on the subject.

10 U.S. Department of Energy, *Environmental Analysis of Synthetic Liquid Fuels* (Washington, D.C.: GPO, 1979), p. 15.

11 National Academy of Sciences, *Rehabilitation Potential of Western Coal Lands* (Cambridge, Mass.: Ballinger, 1974), p. 6.

12 For a review of this research, see U.S. House of Representatives Committee on Science and Technology and Committee on Agriculture, *Agricultural and Environmental Relationships: Issues and Priorities* (Washington, D.C.: GPO, 1979), pp. 47-97.

13 U.S. Environmental Protection Agency, *Environmental Effects of Increased Coal Utilization: Ecological Effects of Gaseous Emissions from Coal Combustion,* Norman R. Glan, ed., June 1978, p. v.

Chapter 10.   Land and the Gasohol Question

1 See, for example, U.S. Council on Environmental Quality, *Solar Energy: Progress and Promise* (Washington, D.C.: GPO, 1978), p. 6.

2 Nigel Smith, *Wood: An Ancient Fuel with a New Future* (Washington, D.C.: Worldwatch Institute, 1981), p. 40.

3 Lester R. Brown, *Food or Fuel: New Competition for the World's Cropland* (Washington, D.C.: Worldwatch Institute, 1980), p. 38.

4 Statement of Deputy Secretary of Agriculture Jim Williams before the Joint Economic Energy Subcommittee of the Joint Economic Committee of the U.S. Congress, March 17, 1980, p. 9.

5 U.S. Department of Energy, *Report of the Alcohol Fuels Policy Review* (Washington, D.C.: GPO, 1979), p. 33.

6 Ibid.

7 U.S. National Agricultural Lands Study, *Final Report* (Washington, D.C.: GPO, 1981), p. 54.

8 Barry Commoner, *The Politics of Energy* (New York: Alfred A. Knopf, 1979), pp. 42-43.

9   *Washington Post,* 3 July, 1979, D-1 (Md).

10 U.S. Congress Office of Technology Assessment, *Gasohol: A Technical Memorandum* (Washington, D.C.: OTA, 1979), p. vi.

11 Kathryn A. Zeimetz, *Growing Energy: Land for Biomass Farms,* Agricultural Economic Report No. 425 (Washington, D.C.: USDA, 1979), p. 31.

12 Statement of Former Secretary of Agriculture Bob Bergland before the Subcommittee on Energy Development and Applications of the Committee on Science and Technology of the U.S. House of Representatives, May 4, 1979, p. 4.

Chapter 11.   Finding the Middleground in Farmland Preservation

1   Amos H. Funk, "A Deed Restriction Proposal," May 1, 1979, mimeo.

2   Edward C. Hussie, in a memorandum to the Honorable Noah W. Wenget, June 15, 1979, pp. 1-2.

3   Curt Harler, "Lancaster County Establishes Agricultural Preserve Board," *Lancaster Farming,* April, 1980, p. 1, 21.

4   Letter to Charles E. Little, May 21, 1980.

5   William J. Duddleson in Robert G. Healy, ed., *Protecting the Golden Shore* (Washington, D.C.: Conservation Foundation, 1978), pp. 10-15.

6   "California Coastal Management," *EPA Journal,* May, 1980, p. 25.

7   The California State Coastal Conservancy, *Report to the Governor and Legislature,* January 1980, p. 4.

8   Ibid., pp. 2-3.

9   Section 31150, Ch. 1441, California Statutes of 1976.

10 *Report to the Governor and Legislature,* p. 22.

11 Ibid., p. 23.

12 Section 31152, Ch. 1441, Cal. Stats. 1976.

13 *Report to the Governor and Legislature,* p. 22.

14   Edward M. Manning and Sandra S. Eddy, *The Agricultural Land Reserves of British Columbia: An Impact Analysis* (Ottawa: Lands Directorate, Environment Canada, 1978), pp. 9-19.

15   E. Neville Ward, *Land Use Programs in Canada: British Columbia* (Ottawa: Lands Directorate, Environment Canada, 1976), pp. 79-80.

16   E. Neville Ward, *Land Use Programs in Canada: Saskatchewan* (Ottawa: Lands Directorate, Environment Canada, 1978), pp. 92-93.

17   Ibid., p. 96.

18   V. Cranmer, *Land Use Programs in Canada: Prince Edward Island* (Ottawa: Lands Directorate, Environment Canada, 1974), pp. 17-20.

19   Ibid., pp. 21-22.

20   Prince Edward Island Land Use Service Centre and the Maritime Resource Management Service Council of Maritime Premiers, *Non-Resident Land Ownership Legislation and Administration in Prince Edward Island* (Ottawa: Lands Directorate, Environment Canada, 1978), pp. 5-13, and p. 77.

21   Ann L. Strong, *Preemption and Farmland Preservation: The French Experience* (Philadelphia: Regional Science Research Institute, 1976), pp. 3-4.

22   Ibid., pp. 16-17.

23   Ibid., p. 19.

24   Ibid., pp. 3-4.

25   Robert A. Lemire, *Creative Land Development* (Boston: Houghton Mifflin, 1979), pp. 55-111.

26   Davis Cherington, "The Need for a Massachusetts Farmland Trust," n.d., pp. 2-3, mimeo.

Chapter 12.   Towards a Farmland Conservancy Concept

 1   This chapter, with minor changes is taken from Charles E. Little, *Middleground Approaches to the Preservation of Farmland* (Washington, D.C.: American Land Forum, 1980).

Chapter 13.   Farmland and the Future

1   Robert E. Coughlin and John C. Keene, "Land Use and the Tax Code," *American Land Forum Magazine* (Summer 1981), p. 22.

2   U.S. National Agricultural Lands Study, *Final Report* (Washington, D.C.: GPO, 1981), p. 91.

3   Robert E. Coughlin and John C. Keene, "Land Use and the Tax Code," p. 18.

Index

W. Wendell Fletcher

W. Wendell Fletcher is a Senior Research Associate with the American Land Forum. Formerly ALF Vice President and General Manager, Mr. Fletcher now devotes full time to research. He has written three major papers for the National Agricultural Lands Study, and has worked on projects from the Department of Housing and Urban Development, the Council on Environmental Quality, and other agencies, and is a frequent contributor to *American Land Forum Magazine*. Prior to joining the ALF, Fletcher was a policy analyst specializing in land use with the Congressional Research Service of the Library of Congress. It was there that he and co-author Charles Little first worked on the analysis of the loss of cropland to urbanization which led to the Jeffords bill and other legislative proposals. Mr. Fletcher is a graduate of Yale University and has an MA in resources management from Syracuse University.

Charles E. Little

Charles E. Little is a founder of the American Land Forum, and its president and editor. He was formerly head of the Natural Resources Section of the Congressional Research Service where he developed analyses and legislative concepts for many land-related issues, including the urbanization of cropland. Prior to his work at the Library of Congress, Little was for two years a senior associate of the Conservation Foundation. Before coming to Washington, he headed the Open Space Institute in New York City (from 1964 to 1970). He has also worked as a book editor (Pergamon Press), a management consultant (Knight, Gladieaux and Smith), and as an advertising man (Foote, Cone and Belding). Besides *The American Cropland Crisis*, he is the author or co-author of three books—*Challenge of the Land, Space for Survival*, and *A Town is Saved* . . .—and is now at work on a fourth, on changes in rural land and life.